THE ROAD TO TENURE

THE ROAD TO TENURE

Interviews, Rejections, and Other Humorous Experiences

Edited by Erin Marie Furtak and Ian Parker Renga

ROWMAN & LITTLEFIELD
Lanham • Boulder • New York • Toronto • Plymouth, UK

Published by Rowman & Littlefield
4501 Forbes Boulevard, Suite 200, Lanham, Maryland 20706
www.rowman.com

10 Thornbury Road, Plymouth PL6 7PP, United Kingdom

Copyright © 2014 by Erin Marie Furtak and Ian Parker Renga

All rights reserved. No part of this book may be reproduced in any form or by any electronic or mechanical means, including information storage and retrieval systems, without written permission from the publisher, except by a reviewer who may quote passages in a review.

British Library Cataloguing in Publication Information Available

Library of Congress Cataloging-in-Publication Data
The road to tenure : interviews, rejections, and other humorous experiences / [14 authors] ; Edited by Erin Marie Furtak and Ian Parker Renga.
p. cm.
Includes index.
ISBN 978-1-4758-0797-4 (cloth) -- ISBN 978-1-4758-0798-1 (pbk.) -- ISBN 978-1-4758-0799-8 (electronic)
1. College teachers--Tenure--Anecdotes. 2. College teachers--Tenure--Humor. 3. American wit and humor--21st century. I. Furtak, Erin Marie, editor of compilation. II. Renga, Ian Parker, editor of compilation.
LB2335.7.R62 2014
378.1'22--dc23
2014001479

For our family, friends, colleagues, and mentors who have joined us along the roads we have traveled

CONTENTS

Acknowledgments	ix
Introduction *Erin Marie Furtak and Ian Parker Renga*	1

I: STARTUP COSTS   5

1 Warning: Scholarship Can Be Hazardous for Your Health   7
  Ian Parker Renga

2 Lucy and the Football: My Search for a Job in a Charlie Brown World   17
  Steve Newton

3 Chocolate Frosting and the Art of Interviewing   27
  Heather M. Bandeen

4 Changing Clothes in the Phone Booth   35
  Jessalynn Strauss

II: OCCUPATIONAL DISSONANCE   41

5 Whose Class Is It Anyway?   45
  Julie C. Mitchell

6 When Homer Simpson Writes Homer's *Iliad*: Preventing Plagiarism while Keeping Your Promotion   51
  Troy Appling

7 How Not to Teach a Class   67
  Andrew Shtulman

8 Publish, Perish, or Apply for Social Security: Reflections on the Tenure Process 81
Logan Greene

9 The Life of the Mind . . . in the Company of Others 89
Amanda Jansen

III: PROFESSORS ARE PEOPLE, TOO 97

10 The Village Idiot 99
Erin Marie Furtak

11 Hot Mess Times Three 109
Hindi Krinsky

12 Who's Pro-creating Now?: Two Sides of Parenting in the Academe 121
Lara Narcisi and Scott Dimovitz

13 How I Got Dismissed from Jury Duty: A Reflection on Philosophy and Public Life 131
Rick Anthony Furtak

About the Editors and Contributors 139

ACKNOWLEDGMENTS

This book would never have come into fruition without the support of Rich Shavelson, who believed in this wacky idea from the beginning, and the Spencer Foundation, which graciously provided a grant to support this project. Marsha Ing, Arjun Chakravarti, Felipe Martinez, Monica Ogra, Noah Feinstein, Rick Furtak, and Andrew Shtulman provided thoughtful reviews of the initial round of abstracts and helped to select the set of essays included in this book. Rick Furtak, Erin's brother, also helped think through initial concepts for the book and suggested language for the original call for essays.

We would also like to thank the Knowles Science Teaching Foundation Research Fellows—Scott McDonald, Beth van Es, Jessica Thompson, Ravit Golan Duncan, Alicia Alonzo, Misty Sato, Indigo Esmonde, April Luehmann, Michelle Cirillo, and Ralph Putnam—for providing ongoing support, humor, and almost unlimited fodder for the manuscript.

INTRODUCTION

Erin Marie Furtak and Ian Parker Renga

Imagine the scene: a county fair with barkers shouting over the din of merry-go-round music and screaming children. Before you is a long, folding table laid out with row upon row of cream pies. On either side of you sit your competitors, and at the judge's request you all clasp your hands behind your backs. At the sound of the bell you begin eating, suppressing your gag reflex as you bite and then swallow mouthful after mouthful of airy meringue and overly sweet filling. As soon as you finish, the empty pie plate is removed and another pie is unceremoniously shoved under your face. You eat and eat, faintly aware of the progress of those surrounding you, but you are focused upon your goal: to eat as many pies as possible. After what seems an interminable amount of eating, the bell rings. You look up, breathing deeply and wiping your face with a damp towel. Your stomach aches at the volume of pie you've just consumed. The sickly taste of excessive cream and crust fills your mouth, and all you long for is a tall glass of water and a rest. When you compare your pile of pie plates to those around you, you realize you've eaten more pie than everyone else. You won! The judge comes up behind you, pats you firmly on the back, and presents you with your award. "For your hard work and determination," he proclaims, "you have earned all the pie you can eat for the rest of your life. Congratulations!" You force a smile as your bowels protest.

This metaphor of the never-ending pie-eating contest has been used to describe the pretenure experience. You plow your way through graduate school and job interviews. Then, if the stars align, you get hired by a college or university, where you break your back writing articles and books, receiving good evaluations on your teaching, and serving the university through endless hours of committee meetings. If you do these things well, you will earn tenure, at which point your "rewards" are heightened expectations for research productivity, teaching quality, and university service. In other words, the prize for eating so much pie is more and more pie.

And as you eat that pie, you maintain a hyped-up, overstimulated state of stressing over this deadline, that review, this lesson plan, that conference call, the presentation—no, not that presentation but this one—the revision, the proofs, the applications, the signatures, the advising sessions, the meetings, the meetings, the meetings, the articles to read that never get read, that chapter you should be working on but can't until after the conference for which you haven't written a proposal and won't until you finish grading these papers, and on and on and on. Each task is checked off to make room for another task, ad infinitum.

Oh, and don't bother asking for cake. You're likely to be told to shut your pie hole. After all, you weren't forced into the pie life: you *chose* it!

When Erin, one of the editors of this book, started her position as assistant professor, she was given several how-to books intended to guide her through this morass, including a short guide to time management, two copies of Robert Boice's classic *Advice for New Faculty Members: Nihil Nimus*; Steven Cahn's *From Student to Scholar*; and to help with writing, *Professors as Writers* and *From Dissertation to Book*.[1] Although lacking the time to fully read these books, Erin skimmed them and gleaned many helpful ideas, such as write every day, limit the time spent on teaching, publish a lot, and try to evade service whenever possible.

With their amassed wisdom, these how-to books offer sound advice, but we find that they inadequately address the humor and drudgery of our daily lives as academics. When you think about it, our profession is a bit amusing. We academics get paid to think. It's our job to relentlessly write and produce tiny, arcane pieces of knowledge that we then fool ourselves into thinking others will find useful. At the same time, we have lives—we travel, we pursue hobbies, and we find partners and start families.

Indeed, what Erin really wanted at the start of her career was a book that captured these personal elements along with the more ridiculous stories of professional life, those she'd often shared over beers and tequila shots with fellow tenure-track friends at conferences. *What do you mean, you can't make your own copies in your building? They seriously have a committee for that? Your graduate student's mother called you to complain?*

Although such evenings were often chased with mornings-after cocktails of Aleve, Tums, double-shot Latte Macchiatos, and Dunkin Donuts, they also offered Erin and her colleagues a release from the professorial pressure cooker by providing opportunities for laughter. Swapping stories and venting brought some measure of comfort and solidarity.

This book reveals the pieces that we find missing from the formal discussion on academic life: the daily grind of our work, our struggles to interface with society at large, and the oppressive rejection wrought by the hands of publishers and students alike. It's early career academics telling the rest of the story, if you will, the stuff that subsumes young scholars yet only comes out in brief hallway encounters or at happy hour gabfests. We see the text as a David-Sedaris-meets-*Nihil-Nimus* collection of essays showcasing the crazy, sometimes darker side of being and becoming professors.[2]

The chapters in this book are organized into three parts, with each part prefaced by a brief introduction by the editors. The parts are loosely grouped around three major dimensions of the academic experience: finding a professional home and identity; making headway in the work; and dealing with the intersection of work and life.

The first part, "Startup Costs," explicates the challenges of entering into academia. In it we hear from individuals who are staring down uncertain futures, trying to both make sense of the professorial role and get hired into tenure-track positions. We start with Ian Renga's description of the physical perils and identity woes of doctoral study. From there we encounter the turbulence of job interviews in the accounts of Steve Newton and Heather Bandeen. Then Jessalynn Strauss shows how, even once a job is achieved, becoming a professor is often nothing short of heroic.

The authors in the second part, "Occupational Dissonance," reveal how each component of the academic trifecta—teaching, writing, and service—presents unique challenges that rarely harmonize. Teaching can be frustrating and, as Julie Mitchell shows through her real syllabus, sometimes humor helps. But often the experience is so agonizing that, as both Troy Appling and Andrew Shtulman reveal, we can only laugh later. Logan Greene shows how publishing can be similarly painful as submitted articles boomerang back. Finally, Amanda Jansen explains how she twists boring service commitments into opportunities for companionship.

In the last part, "Professors Are People, Too," several authors chronicle the strains of moving between life and work. Erin Marie Furtak demonstrates how knowledge garnered through rigorous academic study doesn't always play out as expected in the crucible of the real world. In their chapters, Hindi Krinsky and Lara Narcisi and Scott Dimovitz describe how, for parent-academics, just staying the course can be difficult with children in the picture. And sometimes, as Rick Anthony Furtak shows us, it's hard when our civic responsibilities, like jury duty, require that we check our passion and intellect at the door.

A final warning: If you've picked up this book in order to get ideas on how to succeed in academia, you'll be disappointed because there is little intended advice here. In fact, you're more likely to encounter examples of what *not* to do as a budding academic. It's not all bad news, however, and it should be noted that a palpable aftertaste of satisfaction is evident in all of the chapters. Apparently one can acquire an appreciation for pie (or at least the habits to cope with its side effects). It is our hope that you will see something of yourself in this collection of essays, have a laugh or two, and move on to tackle that next piece of pie on your own road to tenure.

NOTES

1. Robert Boice, *Advice for New Faculty Members: Nihil Nimus* (Boston: Allyn & Bacon, 2000); Steven M. Cahn, *From Student to Scholar: A Candid Guide to Becoming a Professor* (New York: Columbia University Press, 2008); Robert Boice, *Professors as Writers: A Self-Help Guide to Productive Writing* (Stillwater, OK: New Forum Press, 1990); William Germano, *From Dissertation to Book* (Chicago: University of Chicago Press, 2005).

2. Boice, *Advice for New Faculty Members*.

I

Startup Costs

The aspiring scholar starts out as a student with ideas and ambitions, eager to know more and perhaps even hoping to do some good. But to get hired and get ahead this individual must transition from student to scholar, from knowledge consumer to knowledge producer. As the authors in this section illustrate, this new identity often feels funny, like wearing an oversized hat with the promising-yet-inaccurate label *one size fits all*. Harder still is suppressing your doubts during interviews so you can convince prospective employers that the academic hat is definitely a good fit—or, for that matter, convincing yourself (*I'll make it fit!*).

Indeed, going through the rather innocuously labeled "interview process" can be a crazy experience. The smiles and handshakes hide the fact that it's often a process packed with secrecy, subterfuge, ulterior motives, and occasional humiliation, often sold as a two-way "vetting" process whereby universities and applicants alike look for a "good match" (or, as the case may be, a "good enough" match). If you're fortunate, you come out the other side breathless and a little perplexed but with pride intact and a job and new title to burnish your CV. If you're not fortunate, you merely come out perplexed.

Once you've landed that coveted position you'd think that it would be easier to confidently identify yourself as a professor, but often it isn't. Living up to your new title can be difficult. Doubts about entering academia can give way to doubts about how you'll make the experience your own without causing offense. Can you be a professor and still be yourself, or must you reengineer your persona to meet the expectations of students, colleagues, and the institution? What should you ask the students to call you? And what should you wear? There is no single correct answer to these questions, and yet it's still possible to get the answer wrong.

Whether the scholarly transformation occurs during doctoral or postdoctoral study, while interviewing, or after landing the first tenure-track position, it can feel a bit ridiculous, but then, elements of academia can be a little ridiculous. So why subject yourself to the temporal madness, uncertainty, and rigmarole of becoming a professor? Perhaps it is better not to dwell on this question; if junior academics devoted as much time, effort, and energy to the idea of becoming tenured professors as they devote to their ideas, the world would probably have fewer professors.

Thankfully for some of us the passion and the hot cognition of youth triumphs and we willfully, perhaps naively, follow our ideas where they lead us. We choose to become scholars because we trust that it will make a difference and hopefully lead us somewhere worthwhile. As the following authors reveal, that somewhere can be a place populated with bizarre characters, doctor's offices, and strange lodgings (yet sometimes lacking photocopiers).

I

WARNING: SCHOLARSHIP CAN BE HAZARDOUS FOR YOUR HEALTH

Ian Parker Renga

The e-mails from confused undergraduate students often begin, "Dear Professor Renga." "Dear So-and-So," I usually respond, "Please note that I'm just a doctoral student and not a professor. Just 'Ian' will suffice." One time a student wrote back, "Okay Professor Renga, I'll just call you Ian."

The confusion is reasonable. Indeed, I'm not sure that I fully understand my hybrid situation. I teach college courses, attend administrative meetings, and conduct research. My wardrobe is migrating from dresser drawers to closet hangers, and I get out the shoe polish more often than I did as a middle school teacher. But I'm in the infant stages of my dissertation, and the job search has only recently appeared on my radar. To be completely honest, I'm still wavering over whether or not to make academia a full-time career.

Yet professorhood looms, and I feel caught between worlds as the more comfortable moniker of "just Ian" fades while the starchy professional title of "Professor Renga" takes shape. It's like getting my hair cut in slow motion, front to back, so as I reach the midway point of my program it's fair to say that my scholarly ego has a mullet. Curiously, the mullet is the hairstyle of choice for people straddling identities. Consider Labatt-loving Canadians caught between the stodgy European monarchies of the old world and the rock 'n' roll democracy of the new world. Or Kentuckians who find themselves divided between allegiances to the shorn north and wild south. Then there's a young Anakin

Skywalker transforming from the unruly locks of youth to the trimmed efficiency of Jedi Knighthood.[1] We often laugh at the mulletted, but I'd argue that it takes courage to publicly acknowledge one's comfort with a dual identity.

Increasingly I am coming to admire such strength of character as I learn to grin and bear this transitional moment. I am also coming to appreciate the physical strength necessary for surviving the "mind" field of academic work. Indeed, I recently suffered two physical injuries in pursuit of this PhD that have forced me to face my mulletted self, consider who I am and what I'm becoming, and take stock of the whole situation.

EPISODE I: A HOPE FOR HEALTH IN HAND

I was raised in the image of the Rhodes scholar student athlete who maintains a sharp mind by keeping a trim body. But through college I came to see it as a quaint relic of an ivy-covered past when white men, mistaking their racial privilege for inherent talent, actually believed that they could have it all. I'm undoubtedly privileged, though I'm not as naive as my WASPy forebears to believe myself abundantly gifted. Years spent teaching children have revealed that "giftedness" is more widespread and possible, if still latent and undernurtured, than today's self-appointed geniuses would care to admit (ahem, Silicon Valley).

Life is short, and most of us don't have the resources to cultivate a multitude of gifts. Tough choices must be made, so I entered my doctoral program assuming it was reasonable to compromise my body for the sake of my mind. I balked when my dad suggested intramural athletics. I told him that it would interfere with my studies. Besides, I knew that the business school teams would crush my ed school team with our commitment to fairness and equity. I did, however, play some racquetball with a colleague during my first year, but my strategy was to keep him running, so it hardly qualified as a workout.

Later that year, when the graduate school sent out an e-mail for a seminar titled "Coping with Repetitive Stress Disorder," I snickered and thought, *Really? Since when did excessive reading and writing become a health hazard?* I wondered if maybe the university created the course to avoid lawsuits from its gray-haired students. Certainly we young bucks didn't need to cope with anything (except the grumbling of advisors, elders, and especially elder advisors).

Cue the poetic justice: by November of my second year I had typed so much that symptoms of carpal tunnel syndrome developed in my left hand. The tendons in my wrist were inflamed, which severely restricted the movement of my fingers, so the hand was reduced to a perpetually aching claw. The doctor told me that the damage was minimal, but serious caution was advised. For several weeks I had to squeeze out bursts of writing between doses of ibuprofen. I'd kept the injury under wraps, so the situation might have faded into the background if not for a Twilight Zone turn of events that started with a ringing phone. On the other end was my old man, who was calling to pass on the grim news that he'd developed carpal tunnel syndrome. He explained how he'd been wielding power tools while doing extensive yard work when the pain hit him like a Judo chop to the wrist. That's a badass way to get injured, I thought, suddenly ashamed that my injury had resulted from relentlessly pecking on a gummy keyboard. On some level, I felt that I deserved more sympathy than my dad since my injury was tragic given my tender age. Sure, his injury required surgery, but I had wrecked my hand in half the time. Despite these feelings, I bit my tongue and kept the attention on my dad. After all, he had earned it and under far manlier circumstances. To be as tough as him I would have to buy a home with a huge yard, use power tools with fierce determination, and then hide my agonizing pain for decades until the damage demanded attention.

After his operation, I often caught my dad extending and contracting his fingers, turning the hand in careful examination of the surgeon's work. As a baby boomer able to recall the days before computer-aided imagery, I'm sure he was thinking, *Wow, modern medicine is amazing; I should double down on my biotech stock.* As a Gen Xer, too poor to own stock and weaned on *Star Wars*, all I could think of was Luke Skywalker at the end of *The Empire Strikes Back* (1980) admiring his rebuilt hand after losing it to Darth Vader's light saber. Flexing my own injured hand, I was mystified by our eerie hand-to-hand connection and how much it echoed Luke's similar connection to his dad. It occurred to me that, like Luke, I was struggling with my training but hoping for gainful employment in a Jedi temple. Also like Luke, I have a crucial choice to make about my future. And like Darth, my dad made his fateful choice.

A long time ago in a polyester galaxy far, far away, my dad was a doctoral student studying chemistry at the revered Jedi temple in Madison, Wisconsin. He and his mentor made discoveries that pleased the Jedi council, which advanced their respective standings in the order. Shortly after graduating he married my mom and they had me. This turned his attention to an uncertain future, leading him to doubt the Jedi's power to provide him with a competitive paycheck and health benefits. When the Empire (aka big business) came calling, my dad gave into his fear and succumbed to the Dark Side. As a corporate man he had to concede all of his scientific discoveries to his Sith overlords. But in return they gave him a stable salary, swag, and great health insurance. Indeed, my dad's Empire plan paid for his hand surgery and could probably have mechanized his whole body for a low deductible.

Massaging my sore wrist, I contemplated my own uncertain future and felt the temptation of the Dark Side feeding on my fear. On the one hand, there were the good feelings I got from the Jedi's moral righteousness and nonprofit status. But on the other hand, there was the possibility that the injury could get worse and I'd be screwed. It'd be hard enough to type anything worth publishing without having to find clever ways to avoid using the left-hand letters A, S, E, R, and T. With my right hand, I can spell J-U-N-K, which says it all.

Thankfully the pain diminished, if a little more slowly than it would have back in the salad days of my early twenties, and I could maintain my resolve to stay on the Jedi path. Even so, the seeds of fear and doubt were sown, and the next injury proved much less forgiving.

EPISODE II: THE UNIVERSE STRIKES MY BACK

Midway through my third year, I developed an acute case of sciatica, or damage to the large sciatic nerve that carries signals from the spine to the legs and toes. For an academic, the circumstances of the fateful day weren't that unusual: ten hours of sitting, reading, and writing. By evening, I was doubled over with lower back pain. My wife had me do embarrassing yoga poses that foreshadowed what was to come. I tossed and turned all night as the pain crept down my left gluteus and leg, eventually dulling the nerves in my left foot. It was excruciating, like a charley horse that never ends.

In class the next day I gave a presentation, which was the easy part since standing and pacing brought relief. Sitting through the other presentations was the rough part. I'm sure my grimaces and twitchy shifting were seen as rude, but this seemed preferable to proclaiming aloud, "Sorry everyone, I'm suffering from a nerve malady common in pregnant women!"

Perhaps you're skeptical that the cause of the sciatica was sitting. I was, too, but sitting is not a natural position for humans and can have deleterious health effects, especially when done excessively.[2] This is bad news for scholars, since academia is the quintessential information-age profession: it's ass-in-chair work. When people ask me what I do, I feed them a line about making the world a better place. But really, I mostly sit in front of a computer reading, grading, and bouncing e-mails. I doubt Bono will call.

In a cruel twist, an academic has to get up from the computer and exercise to enable lengthier and more productive ass-sitting. I can do this, but it takes trickery, like taking a brisk midday walk to get lunch. With exercise for exercise's sake I feel like a hamster, or worse, a tool. The huffing, puffing, and sweating reminds me that my body is, in the crudest sense, just a machine. Exercise draws unwanted attention to my body, so I tend to ignore it.

Sciatica got my attention. The doctor surmised that my weeklong push to renovate our bathroom had triggered it. Since I tend to slouch while I type, the excessive sitting had weakened my back muscles. My brash embrace of the home-improvement project pushed those muscles to their limits, and the spinal discs, poorly supported, slipped a little, pinching the sciatic nerve. In the throes of pain I regretted letting it get that far, but the brashness had felt so refreshing. I had ditched my computer to heft toilets and contort my six-foot frame into the tiny vanity precisely because I wanted a change of pace from academic drudgery. More significantly, I wanted proof that I was more than some guy who, if he were an action figure, would come packaged with a laptop, office chair, headphones, and a stale cup of coffee. Indeed, an identity crisis had been brewing that this incident brought front and center.

During the bathroom renovation I donned my most wretched clothes and escaped from the world of digitized data by crunching numbers with a stubby pencil on the back of an envelope. I eschewed careful and systematic reasoning by brazenly making shit up. I made repeated trips to Lowe's to purchase the various pieces of my plumbing puzzle and then spent hours on the bathroom floor fitting them together.

Intellectual work is mailed into the void, but here I could sit upon my glistening new porcelain throne and behold the fruits of my labor. When guests came over and asked to use the bathroom, I casually referred them down the hall and then waited with heart racing, a triumphant post-potty exchange taking shape:

"I love the bathroom. Great craftsmanship. It must have taken you a long time."

"Oh, thanks. It was no big deal. A side project, really."

"No, seriously, it's amazing. I'm telling all the cool people to come check it out."

"You don't have to do that. Besides, my bathroom is for all people."

In reality, they'd emerge and, if they said anything, it'd be about how pleasant the hand soap smells. ("I agree. The lavender is soothing. And you can get that brand at most grocery stores.") It never felt appropriate to further inquire into their restroom experience, so I'd let it go.

The hard, physical work awoke something within me, an inner yearning to be more down to earth, a real craftsman less constrained by his mind. In football terms, I wanted to be more like New York Giants quarterback Eli Manning and less like his older brother Peyton, who used to helm my hometown Indianapolis Colts. Both Mannings are known for their stout work ethics, but Peyton's version is headier and often labeled by football pundits as "academic." Eli's ethic is more of an aw-shucks variety, and I have an easier time imagining him doing his own home renovation. He gets results on the field, too. Days after I finished up the bathroom he succeeded in taking down the New England Patriots in the Super Bowl (wait for it Pats fans) for the second time. As the junior Manning hoisted the Lombardi trophy, I toasted him with a cold one. I even asked for an Eli jersey for my birthday.

After finishing the bathroom, life seemed swell. But the universe can sniff out frauds; it knew I was really Peyton parading around in his brother's uniform, so it brought the pain. I hobbled to the doctor hoping that the cool students would take my dragging left leg for a pimp limp. My penance began the moment the doctor asked me to bend over and touch my toes. I formed a lower case *r* instead of the desired cursive *l*. The doctor kindly informed me of my ailment and signed me up for weekly physical therapy. I was now an advanced graduate student taking mandatory remedial gym class.

Each of my slights was punished in kind. Since I had dissed working out, I was forced to wear gym shorts and cross-trainers to the therapy sessions. And since I had thumbed my nose at research I was to partake in what my physical therapist referred to as a "data-driven" recovery. Each session started and ended with taking precise measurements of my lameness and entering the numbers into a computer. I also assumed rather suggestive stretching positions and routinely exposed my damaged cheek for probing. For several weeks I was even strapped to a modern version of a medieval rack. Looking up at the tiled ceiling with its star field of tiny holes, my body subjected to the therapeutic cruelty of two opposing forces, I pondered life's essential contradictions: yin and yang, body and mind, and Eli and Peyton.

The humiliation didn't stop at the doctor's office. At home I had to throw out my old office chair and replace it with a big blue exercise ball (also known as a "birthing ball"). It was that or a grown-up version of a booster seat. The ball is supposed to be good for my posture and a way to exercise my back and abdomen. It's fine in this capacity, but it clashes horribly with the rich merlot walls and Western-themed art of my office. Sitting on this giant balloon, I've had to discard any fantasies of wearing spurs while writing my dissertation. Occasionally when getting up, I knock the ball into the wall, and it makes a "boink" sound that evokes memories of my dodgeball days and reminds me of the cold, hard fact that I'd be terrible at dodgeball now.

Indeed, the blue ball shatters the illusion that I'm workingman tough, a wooly blend of Ernest Hemingway, Teddy Roosevelt, and Pablo Picasso. Its conspicuous gym smell and workout video appearance reminds me that I belong to a sissified era. Ernest, TR, or Pablo probably never rolled around on a large rubber ball in gym shorts grunting and groaning. And if they could see me on the ball? Oh, the humiliation. They'd barge in, TR's face flush with disgust, his eyes squinting to shut out the sight. "You there! Young man. For God's sake! Get off that thing and join us for a long jaunt in the hills to walk off that ridiculous injury!"

Better that I imagine being discovered by the Manning brothers, who almost certainly wear gym shorts and train on exercise balls. "Just a few more reps!" they'd call out together, Eli patting me on the shoulder. "You can do it, champ!"

EPISODE III: RELEASE DATE UNKNOWN

Some days the doctoral clock ticks by ominously, the larger tenure clock ready to take its place, while the pieces of a more familiar self are shorn away so a new self can emerge. My injuries have revealed this new self to be more vulnerable than expected. Faculty mentors keep asking me what I'm most passionate about as a scholar—what drives me. In the midst of setbacks, when darker thoughts haunt me, the best answer I can muster is that I'm driven to avoid failure—a sound motivation, I suppose, but hardly nourishing.

I walk precariously between two possible story lines. One is a story of redemption where the aspiring academic quits licking his wounds, applies a craftsman's sensibility to his innermost passions, and completes a hard-earned transformation into Professor Renga. The other is a story of disappointment where the aspiring academic fails to heed the warning signs and squanders his opportunity, staying "just Ian," the mulletted wanderer, doomed to drift aimlessly in a fraying Eli Manning jersey.

It has been suggested that I seek out well-worn theories that address the good life and self-improvement. I'm told that, like a mirror held askew reflecting back an unfamiliar view, a good theory can offer a fresh perspective on the question, *Who am I?* Okay, but no amount of self-analysis can convince me that my inner mullet is worth keeping.

Indeed, as I lace up my cross-trainers and gaze inward, I'm reminded of the well-tested folk theory "shit happens." Bizarre and unexpected things inevitably occur, incidents that rattle one's sense of confidence and self-control. The challenge is to avoid letting the shit mess with your head. Again I turn to Luke Skywalker: he starts his journey believing that the face of evil is clear until it hits the fan and that face is his father's (and possibly his own). Rather than running away to Dagoba to hide away in Yoda's hermit hole, he finds a measure of peace in the contradictions of his evolving identity and bravely charts his own path forward.

Were I to follow Luke's example, I would quit fretting over my scholarly transformation and embrace the challenges and inconsistencies that it presents. I would wear my Eli Manning jersey while rooting for his brother Peyton (sounds doable). I would patiently sport my inner mullet while exercising atop the big, blue ball (perhaps a little harder but also doable). And I would sign e-mails to students as "Professor Renga" knowing I'm still "just Ian." All right, I can't do this last one yet. I still have a dissertation to write.

sigh

My back aches just thinking about it.

NOTES

1. Judge for yourself by Googling the stinker-of-a-film *Star Wars Episode II: Attack of the Clones* (2002) when no one is looking over your shoulder.

2. Several studies have linked "sedentary behavior" with increased health risks, though claims are challenged on methodological grounds. For a comprehensive review of the research, see the following: Alicia A. Thorp, Neville Owen, Maike Neuhaus, and David W. Dunstan, "Sedentary Behaviors and Subsequent Health Outcomes in Adults: A Systematic Review of Longitudinal Studies, 1996–2011," *American Journal of Preventive Medicine* 41, no. 2 (2011): 207–15.

2

LUCY AND THE FOOTBALL

My Search for a Job in a Charlie Brown World

Steve Newton

The year before I went up for tenure at my old institution I lost my English professor job, which led to a year floundering and flopping around in what became an increasingly desperate job search. I was forty-seven, single, and without a girlfriend or children. I applied to somewhere around 125 schools and ended up wandering like a hangdog-restless shade around the country, woefully looking for work.

I would eventually find it and achieve tenure at my current institution in New Jersey. But it did not come easy. Like good ol' Charlie Brown, I kept trying to kick the football while Lucy repeatedly pulled it away at the last second, sending me flying up in the air, heels over head, in a cloud of dust and disappointment. I would get myself all psyched up, put on my best game face for the interview or the in-class teaching demonstration or the meetings with the dean and department chair and president; try to sustain this readiness through the whole rigmarole of taking the taxi out to the airport, flying somewhere far away, meeting a bunch of new people, having meetings and lunches and dinners that could last as long as three days but usually two, and sometimes just one; and fly back home and expectantly wait for a call that might change my life for the better, only to be told, "You didn't get it." And that is if they even bothered to call.

At one school in Texas I was having lunch with a group of professors—all male—in a faculty lounge. One thoughtful professor brought in some homemade chili for my lunch. It was very, very spicy, so much so that I was getting flustered by the amount of sweat showing on my rather prominent forehead. Things got spicier when the department chair started telling stories about going to stripper bars. Seriously? How should I react? Like one of the good ole boys? Call them out on their extraordinarily inappropriate behavior? Or perhaps try to act like I didn't have steam coming out of my ears while I was mopping my forehead and trying to act all nonchalant.

That night at dinner the wife of the red-hot-chili professor asked me why I didn't have a wedding ring on—code for *Are you gay?*—and then asked about my ethnic background and religion—code for *Are you Jewish?* Both of these questions were outrageously out of line, not to mention illegal. By sending in a spouse, maybe the search committee thought they were being clever. After dinner we went out to a bar and listened to a country-rock band and drank a lot of beer. Yee haw, professor! Welcome to Texas, where English department chairs joke about lap dances with job candidates from New York City at lunch.

At another school, during a big group interview, a graduate student displayed his recently acquired—and obviously proudly so—limited grasp of arcane literary theory in his formulation of a question to me. It was an awkward moment. Especially when I asked him to please repeat the question in English, or something to that effect. My answer did not go over well, and the little tête-à-tête between the grad student and me probably ensured that I would not get hired there. Unfortunately, after that high-toned lit theory tempest in a teapot, I still had another whole day and night of meetings and dinners to go through. Hard to keep your game face on when you realize you are now food for the crows in the eyes of the hiring committee.

At yet another school, in my departmental committee interview, I mentioned an article written by an obscure but sort of well-known academic. This elicited a kind of creepy, nervous, shared look across the table between two faculty members. I left thinking, *huh? What in the world is going on here?* Then later that day I happened to see the CV of this well-known academic lying out on a desk. What? Really?? I confronted the woman who had been showing me around, and she would not comment on it, but it turned out that this guy did, in fact, get the job and had already been to campus and been interviewed by the time I was there. I was, come to find out, a candidate who was just going through the motions: the hapless job candidate who they fly down and flirt with to satisfy their hiring guidelines. Yep, it happens. And it sucks when it happens to you. It's much worse when you figure out the scam while you are still in the process of being interviewed.

It was after these and other exhausting and borderline traumatizing episodes that I traveled out to a small town in Nevada, which I'll call Oakville, for a job interview and another chance to try and kick the football. Surely, eventually, someone would let me kick the damn thing. Right?

* * *

This was the first time I was going to be in this part of the country since 1970, so flying over the Rockies was both adventure and palimpsest. We went over range after range of snow-capped mountains, plateaus, arroyos, and buttes, and as much as it was all spectacular, it was really more like I wanted it to be spectacular, or else I was going to have to find a new word, because the actual, real-time experience of flying over the mountains was a letdown. Things really do flatten out the farther up and away you get. Distance provides perspective but robs power.

The approach to Salt Lake City, however, was more of what I had been hoping for. This was an emptiness with jagged fields of looming sunlight on rocks and snow. The metro jukebox blast of NYC, beating with collective hive pulse and housed in towers of light, was now far behind. I was face-to-face with a stark, wind-scoured, skull-rattling, rocky face that stares balefully up at clear stars through the western night everlasting. I spent one night in the city and took a bus to Oakville, Nevada, the next day. It was a spectacular trip in some ways, and it took me through some of the emptiest, most desolate country I had ever seen.

A fellow from the office of Academic Support Services, whom I will call Cody, picked me up from the bus station in his four-wheel-drive truck. On the way I asked him about the identity of some distant mountains. Without missing a beat he snapped that I was the geography expert; I ought to be telling him what those mountains were. Wait, what? First off, where is the famed western hospitality? And second, why does he think that I am a geography professor? All of this was happening very fast, and I was being forced to improvise, and what came out was pretty lame, a series of stammers and strangled looks that communicated I was not anything remotely close to an expert on western mountain ranges, and I had not a smidgen of a blind idea why he referred to me as the "geography expert." This fact was immaterial, of course, or should have been by any decent standards that I know of, because even if I had been the expert he thought I was, this would have been the worst possible way to greet a guest and potential future employee of the college.

As soon as we established that I was the English professor, we moved on to talking about my lodgings. I make no claim to psychic powers. I leave those matters to Dionne Warwick and the rest of the snake-oil soothsayers on the psychic hotline. As we approached town, however, I began having uncomfortably vivid moments of acute anxiety and unusual clarity regarding the possibility of being forced to stay with strangers during my stay in Oakville.

I had first spoken to the hiring committee on a conference call for about an hour. They had wanted me to come out immediately for an on-campus interview as a finalist. Unfortunately, this didn't allow enough time to get a reduced rate on the plane ticket, and the price was prohibitive. After a few days I got another phone call. One of the deans knew someone who knew someone who had used a discount ticket agency, and could I check it out? Yes, I could, of course I could and did. I bought the tickets, did my part, but after all this I was informed that, well, there was a mining expo in Oakville that week and there was no way that I was going to get a room within two hundred miles of town. They would take care of everything, though. I was not to worry. When I got out to Oakville, I would have a room for the three-day visit, and I was not, repeat not, to worry. Right. Like trying to tell the armadillo not to cross the road. So I was not surprised when Cody informed me that I would be staying at someone's home. He said that it was a bed and breakfast, but somehow I knew that this was going to be one of those totally impossible situations. Of course, the concept of impossible is, in most cases, entirely relative. If one really needs to adjust, one finds the resources to do so. The problem arises when the psychic energies that you have at your disposal are running low, and at this point in the trip the needle was pointing precariously close to empty. My worst fears about the prospective Oakville situation seemed to be coming true.

I would be staying with some former professors from the college who had a whole separate apartment in the rear of their house. I would have my own entrance so I could come and go as I pleased. The drive to the house did not take long, as the town was very small, and after making a brief stop on campus, walking around for about fifteen minutes, and visiting Cody's office to retrieve something or other, we were soon parking on a nice, tree-lined, quiet street of immaculate upper-middle-class homes with emerald green lawns and leafy trees. We walked across the lawn up to the door. As soon as the woman of the house opened the door, everything quickly changed. Cody didn't know her. He had been misinformed. There was no wing in the back. There was only a bedroom upstairs in an otherwise entirely private home, with no special accommodations whatsoever for boarders. I would be taking meals with the family if I so desired.

This meant that in between being grilled by the search committee and giving a job talk, I would be sitting around in someone else's living room or den, in a strange town, making small talk with strangers. The minutes would tick slowly by while I roasted over the hot coals. I would be coming and going for three days out of someone's kitchen, some anonymous stranger in a town I didn't know. But what could I say at this point? I had traveled all the way across the country to try to make these people like me and want to hire me, not to act like some hypertense, crazed, NYC, cigarette-holder-using, beret-wearing, downtown literary salon snob who didn't find these meager chintz and veneer, vulgar knick-knack accommodations acceptable. The problem, however, was not that I didn't find the lodgings acceptable—they were much nicer than I was used to. The issue here was privacy.

Maybe this lodging situation shouldn't have been a big deal, and in many ways you would be absolutely on the mark in wondering why I was turning what could have been a perfectly manageable situation into an impossibly snarled inferno of conflict and difficulty. But after all of these campus visits, I had reached my limit. I could sense that my fate was sealed. This situation was clearly one that was worth going into the surf over.

Having fulfilled his duties, Cody split this little scene of misery and discomfort, leaving me with the suburban Nevada hausfrau for the remainder of the afternoon. I stashed my bags in the room upstairs and took my leave out the kitchen door into the side yard, saying that I wanted to wander around the town and maybe get a better look at the campus. The college was not far away. It only took me about ten minutes to walk.

The campus wasn't a very big place, and it didn't take long for me to get the layout. I asked a man in the empty snack bar how to get to the humanities building, and it turned out it was right next door. In short order I was navigating my way through a maze of offices looking for the woman with whom I'd set up the logistics for this visit. I talked with her along with several women on the English department and humanities office staff. It appeared that there was a dramatic difference between the way that these women perceived the severity of the housing situation and the way that I saw things. They moved slow, talked slow, and had very pleasant demeanors, but it was all in a weird sort of grandmother-from-hell kind of way.

It took some doing, but I finally convinced them that I really did need to speak with someone higher up in the chain of command about my housing situation if there was nothing that they were going to do about it. The excuse they gave me—that there was a mining convention in town—just wasn't convincing. My guess was that these people had just not tried very hard to find a vacancy. They had found me a room, which they apparently thought was good enough, and as far as they were concerned, that would do. There was nothing else that needed to be done, and certainly no more that needed to be said. That was, of course, until they had me hopping around in their office like Daffy Duck on speed, a flabbergasted flibbertigibbet with clots of hair sticking out, spittle flying, and cerebral veins throbbing and bulging so tightly that it looked like I was about to spout a gusher of bright arterial blood, a pulsing geyser squirting from the dome of my imposingly large forehead. Okay, that's a little bit over the top, but I think, dear reader, that you might get the picture.

The entire office staff seemed to have lived in Oakville their whole lives, knew every miner and casino doll; every Sunday morning bootlegger and back-alley whorehouse; where to find the best pair of boots and who could fix your rototiller; and who to call if your sunflowers wilted or your goldfish went belly up. Yet when they were faced with the challenge of finding a stressed-out Yankee a motel room, a simple enough, rather straightforward matter, or so it would seem, they decided rather quickly that the best thing to do would be to shunt me down the hall to the office of the grand poobah. It was the one place in the building where everyone agreed that authority was gathered, concentrated, perhaps even in a refined, distilled form. And it was precisely this imperial, awe-filled presence that was ostensibly going to provide the solution for my problems, a set of daunting issues that so far had eluded the meager abilities of the Grange Hall grannies that answered the phone in the English department. These women seemed incapable of helping me out and thinking independently, but the one thing they could do when faced with a little kerfuffle caused by an out-of-towner, was to pass the buck to the boss, some unlucky bureaucrat whom they couldn't stand the sight of, though they surely would never put it quite that way. The newly appointed academic vice president must have fit the bill a little too perfectly.

He certainly looked the part, a classic example of the hapless newcomer filled with self-importance and gravitas, when it is clear to everyone from the janitor to the gym teacher that he is nothing more than a self-involved blowhard without a clue as to how things are actually done around the college. This meant, of course, that he was the only person who would actually help me out. This turned out to be a small but very important bit of good news in an otherwise desolate landscape. I seemed to be the embodiment of New York City, mister-know-it-all-East-Coast-smarty-pants professor, and I had to have things just the way I wanted them, didn't I? Well, we will just have to see about that, won't we, Professor?

I don't like to think of myself as being inordinately concerned with fashion, but that doesn't mean that I'm not. It just means that I don't like to dwell on the likelihood that I'm every bit as one-dimensional as everybody else. Probably more so, truth be told. I think that this rather unattractive, shallow aspect of my personality has become magnified since I have been living in New York City, where one is constantly in contact with people speaking to each other in the language of clothes. This sartorial web of meaning is too complicated to decipher much of the time, too intricately woven to extract individual threads, or at least it has become so in the fragmented tessellation of postmodernity, where cowboy boots and Levis are routinely paired with a polo shirt and blazer, often complemented by multiple facial and body piercings and elaborate tattoos—and the men wear even stranger combinations.

Maybe I was just stretched a little bit too tight at that moment, but when I walked into the office of the vice president of the college and saw that he was wearing a maroon blazer, well, the fuses started to blow by the box full. The problem here, the situation that made this little meeting so delicate, so fraught with peril, was that along with interviewing for the job of my dreams, the culmination of all of my fantasies, and the fulfillment of my wildest desires, I also had to find a place to stay for the next couple of nights that wasn't a nightmare on Oakville street. And I had to get this guy to make it happen. This recently appointed midlevel rump smoocher and paper stacker was wearing a bizarre maroon blazer made from some stiff Wal-Mart polyester fabric woven from space-age fibers in a former shipyard in Gdansk; a regulation real-estate-salesman white plastic belt complemented by a JC Penney open-collar, see-through material, off-white dress shirt; and a short wide tie with a splotchy pattern that looked like crow guano dripping down the front in green and white gouts and speckles, or perhaps the canvas of an abstract expressionist chipmunk with projectile diarrhea. He was dressed, in other words, like a combination TV preacher, used car salesman, tight-ass Rotarian, and five-county propane distributor in East Jesus, Arizona—either that or a cop, guidance counselor, or principal from some wise-ass teen movie, the guy you know from the first reel is going to wind up exposed as a dork in front of the whole school.

Mr. Discount Store didn't have any more of an idea than anyone else about where I might stay. He did, however, listen and did not dismiss me as some hopped-up Gotham lunatic, as everyone else had done west of the Pecos. Perhaps it was because he had recently moved to Nevada from New Hampshire. Maybe he saw me as a kind of kindred spirit. Then again maybe he just saw a guy who needed some help. And maybe there are people who try to help out if they can, regardless of what's in it for them. This runway model for the polyester and Geritol set made a few phone calls and found me a room without much trouble at all.

Looking back I am a bit disappointed in my inability to see past the vice president's fashion faux pas, but at the time I just wanted a room in a no-tell motel at the dust-buster end of the world that would shade my tattered dreams with seedy sheets and a stained carpet. A man needs to have a place to go where he can feel spiritually at home from time to time, after all. In a move that would have pleased the yee-haw Texas profs, the VP had put me in a casino, one conveniently located in the center of town, within easy staggering distance of the adult entertainment district.

I was feeling like I was just this side of the Big Rock Candy Mountain, where you boil in oil the inventor of toil, never have to wash your socks, and little streams of alcohol come running through the rocks. Such is the mythology of the West and the iconography of the hobo anyhow, at least as it once was immortalized in popular song: the vagabond child saint walking the distant reaches of the buffalo-scented purple sage and then heading off for the cloud-shrouded ridges of blue firs with Johnny Appleseed.

Anyhow, these were the kinds of thoughts I was having back then, bouncing around back and forth between one extreme and the other, between dream and nightmare, hausfrau and blackjack dealer. And so I was in a fairly sorry state by the time I found myself shaking hands with the hiring committee, comprised of what were apparently bored, put-upon, resentful small-town academics, who seemed to have very little interest in the job-selection process that meant so very much to me. They didn't even pretend being interested. Something felt like an ending during this process, as if the theme music was already playing and the curtain was starting to come down. It may be that this is just something that I imagine now, looking back, but that is the way that I remember it.

* * *

Eventually it was over, and before I knew it I was zooming along in the hotel airport shuttle in Salt Lake City, on my way home, about to fly back across the country. I still had a long way to go before I would be back in New York City, but that was okay. For the time being, I was still in Utah, surrounded by squawking sea gulls, white pelicans, mirage-covered salt flats, and distant mountains capped with snow and violet shadows.

It's no surprise to me that I was not hired in Oakville, or in Texas for that matter. I have been part of enough hiring committees by now to know how hard it can be to feign enthusiasm and how easily candidates can misinterpret perfectly innocent situations. Because that is finally what wound up happening to me as a result of a year of running around the country looking for work and getting turned down time and time again, believing that Lucy was going to hold the football still for me, even though she had pulled it away every time before.

I take full responsibility. It turns out that I was the one misinterpreting things, bringing my own problems to places where they didn't belong, although in my defense, it got kind of rough out there. It sure did. But in the end, after all of this job search insanity, all the quasi-operatic drama, I was finally able to kick the football. It is still sailing over the trees today.

3

CHOCOLATE FROSTING AND THE ART OF INTERVIEWING

Heather M. Bandeen

I escape to the restroom to perform my mid-interview once-over. Quickly smoothing the front of my dress and leaning into the mirror, I check for food in my teeth and in my hair. Sadly, both happen quite frequently. Finding nothing, I take a deep breath and then step back to get the full view of myself. I look good. My trusty black polyester dress is channeling a cross between Ruth Bader Ginsburg and Meg Ryan. I am rocking this interview.

And, then I notice it. My feet start to shake in my sensible yet snazzy shoes. I lean forward to peer at my neckline. I see the tiny white tag peeking out from my collar. My dress is on backward. I have been sitting at my morning interview with my dress on backward. This is not good. Oh, well. Dressing one's self was not in the job posting (sigh).

This moment perfectly captures my last year of graduate school. Most days, my perception was that life was good when, unfortunately, that was not always the case. During those final months, I was confronted by an array of inevitable blunders. These blunders became the hallmark of my existence as I frantically finished my dissertation, battled graduation demons, and planned my escape—to more of the same: an Academic Job.

I was not the only one. You can spot a graduate student in that final stretch from miles away. We know our own. We drink unhealthy amounts of coffee. We binge on clearance-aisle, economy-sized bags of candy. We have a complete disregard for any semblance of personal hygiene.

Before my doctoral degree, I was pretty "pulled together." I had quirks, but they were of the charming, Mary Tyler Moore variety. There were my clothes. My socks never matched; so, I wore boots. And my car. It was a disaster; so, I parked far away. And my eating habits. I ate peanut butter straight from the jar; so, I did not host dinner parties. In my former life, I tucked these small secrets away, and no one knew. In grad school, they grew. They procreated. They lived large for all to see. What did that mean for finding an academic job? Well, the thought of dressing up and venturing into the world to convince others that they should pay me seemed laughable. Not that I was laughing.

My job search process became a dance of late-night futility. I typed cover letters and lost myself in the syntax of a single sentence for hours. During moments of brief respite, I would stray to websites with cute spring outfits. You know the ones that feature glossy-haired models with tiny waistlines. Inevitably, these images would fail to make me feel better so I would wander to the bathroom for a pep talk with the mirror. These pep talks often ended with a bleak return to my laptop, holding a jar of chocolate frosting. Small comforts.

Around this time, I met my now husband. His name is Jason. He was inexplicably attracted to me in my "drain state." During our courtship, we wrote epic e-mails to each other and, eventually, procrastinated ourselves into dating.[1] Somehow, Jason and I met when we were at identical points in our programs: the hellish end. Our first date consisted of odd conversations like, "You're cute. How do you feel about New York? Wanna live there in six months?"

We wrestled with the all-too-common job search dilemma of the "two body problem." This is a common issue that partners face when they meet in grad school and then, ridiculously, decide that they would like to live in the same city. We approached this problem like unabashed nerds and created a virtual map of academic job postings that stretched from Boston to Honolulu. We then calculated driving times between institutions and speculated about hiring time lines. This data gave rise to an elaborate spreadsheet. I soon found that the universe does not take kindly to spreadsheets.

In the beginning, I was excited for every interview invitation. Yes, I was cozy in my sweatpants, chatting with my bathroom mirror. I still

CHOCOLATE FROSTING AND THE ART OF INTERVIEWING

had quite a bit of chocolate frosting to eat. But I was ready to contribute to the universe again. Admittedly, though, I wasn't in my best interviewing shape. My formerly sparkling small-talk skills were dull. When I entered grad school in my twenties, I was "hip."[2] Now, I did not have cable and listened to copious amounts of NPR. Also, my professional "look" at this point was marginal, at best. To save money, I allowed the local beauty school to practice on my hair. The idea had merit, but it led to my mouse-brown hair becoming purple-black. I had a Goth-head on a Midwestern-frosting-filled body.

The truth is, even when the proverbial cards are in your favor, interviews represent a difficult situation. No matter what anyone tells you, you will be nervous. Meanwhile, everyone you meet is squeezing you into a very busy schedule. And, frankly, some will not be terribly interested in you or anything you have to say. Most faculty members that I met were kind and welcoming. For this, I was grateful. There were a few disappointments: The person who fell asleep during my job talk.[3] The person who repeatedly complained about his students, by saying, "These kids would never make it into the Ivy League!" The person who taunted me with an impromptu game of guess-my-personal-theory-of-the-universe. The person who said, "Looks like your next appointment is in building A with Bob. Good luck finding it."

By December, Jason and I had each received a couple of job offers. We felt confident and excited. The possibilities that we dared to think about during our late-night work sessions were coming true. Loans would be paid off. Perhaps I could even afford a spring outfit.

We were advised to turn down these early offers and wait for even better ones. So, we did. I was elated. I sailed into the holidays with hope. Then January 2009 arrived, and the world's economy tanked. No academic budgets. No jobs. No paid student loans. No spring outfits. I broke out my stash of chocolate frosting and returned to my bathroom mirror.

A few colleges did contact me in spite of this economic woe. When I received my first interview invitation during the fall semester, I was nervous. This anxiety inspired me to become a thirtysomething Girl Scout. I prepared for days ahead of time. I planned all of my outfits and even tucked snacks into my pockets. Locusts be damned. I was ready for anything. Yet by the spring thaw, I was contemplating the possibility of a failed job search. My dissertation was hitting multiple snags. And I was coordinating major life decisions with someone I met three months ago. The result? I became, well, less proactive with my preparation.

One interview continues to stand out in my memory. As per usual, this interview in small-town Midwest USA included a series of one-on-one interviews with faculty members and a couple of presentations. My adventure began as I threw my Ginsburg/Ryan black polyester dress and related interview accouterment into a suitcase. I also packed my laptop and flash drive with drafts of my presentations. I planned to complete my final edits during the plane ride and make copies of my handouts that evening. My first night's schedule included an airplane flight, a rental car, a hotel check-in, and a dinner interview with faculty. What could be easier?

The flight went smoothly. My edits were nearly complete. I picked up my rental car. Then, I punched the address into my GPS contraption, which I always bring with me. My GPS contraption has a voice named Samantha. She and I have a love-hate relationship. She is bossy and protests loudly when I stop for snacks. She is particularly petulant when I stop at Dairy Queen. (How does she know?) Our exchanges usually go a little something like this:

> Heather: Now don't be angry, Samantha. I need to stop for ice cream.
>
> Samantha: Missed turn. Turn left now. Rerouting. Rerouting. Turn right now. Rerouting.
>
> Heather: Hold on, this will only take a minute.
>
> Samantha: Rerouting. Rerouting! Rerouting!!
>
> Heather: Oh, my God! I totally deserve this and you know it!

On this particular afternoon, I pulled out of the airport and thought, *This state is made for speed.* No matter where I looked, I saw flat landscape with herds of bored cattle and an occasional horse cameo. I hit the gas and listened to a doleful Samantha say, small-town Midwest USA . . . forty-eight miles. Her screen revealed one blue line. No turns. No diversions. One straight, unfettered drive through absolute nothingness.

As I pulled into town, I passed a handful of nondescript buildings and quickly located the hotel. I absent-mindedly practiced my interview-at-any-moment mumblings for that night's dinner: "Hi, I'm Heather. Great to meet you! I am excited about your college because of your mission, your international programs, and your obvious love of dairy." I pulled into a parking spot and hopped into the chilly evening to make my way to the hotel's front lobby. It was covered in retro, flowered wallpaper and was also completely empty. The deserted front desk offered a shiny bell. After repeated rings of the bell, the front desk clerk appeared and handed over an actual key to my room. I slipped it into my pocket. It felt heavy. I threw my luggage into the room and then found the small nearby restaurant with a friendly group of faculty. They warned me that the next day's schedule was packed and would begin very early.

After a couple of hours of frantic work, I climbed behind the wheel of the rental car with my flash drive in hand. I was ready to print my handouts and get some sleep. I punched C-O-P-Y S-T-O-R-E into my GPS contraption. Samantha remained obstinately silent. After a minute or so, I heard, "Searching for satellites." I glared at her and muttered, "You lost them . . . again? There are hundreds up there!" Finally, she yielded with two words: "None available." I gulped and paused to think. Maybe "copy store" was too specific? I tried C-O-P-Y. Again, two words: "None available." Then, I slowly typed S-T-O-R-E. (At this point, I am ashamed to admit that I also pleaded in a whimpery voice.) Clearly and calmly, Samantha enunciated two different words: "Super Walmart." I sat quietly, staring ahead. She said nothing more. Her screen glowed while I listened to myself breathe. Pulling from every ounce of remaining energy, I fended off an overpowering inclination to throw a tantrum and pitch her right out of the window. Finally, I heaved a sigh and resolutely turned the key in the car's ignition. For the first time, I looked up. The streets were deserted. I drove in the darkness until I saw the glow of retail lights surrounded by nothingness. It was becoming painfully clear that I was in trouble.

Super Walmart was my only hope. As I walked through the swishing glass doors, I found the store to be as deserted as the streets. The few loitering employees seemed startled to see me. They shrugged at the sight of my flash drive and told me that they did not know of anywhere to print "this late." I thanked them. Then, I began to curse under my breath on the walk across the empty parking lot. I needed these handouts for my presentation. I had to find a way.

My next brilliant idea was to visit every hotel in the area to see if they might have a business center. I grabbed my GPS and desperately typed in "hotel." For the next hour, Samantha led me to a series of remote roadside motels in a somewhat judgmental tone. Nothing resembling technology was found at any of these locations. A few miles out of "town," I stumbled upon a small motel with a few cars out front. A beleaguered front desk clerk took pity on me and allowed me to use a computer that actually whirred and coughed as it printed. Aha! I now had one printout. I felt powerful. I effusively thanked the clerk, who kept looking at me and shaking her head.

My head hit the pillow that night with exhaustion and relief. I would just use the copier that I had spotted at the dark Super Walmart customer service desk in the morning. So the next day, I woke up early with an hour allotted to make copies before my breakfast interview. I leapt from the bed, turned around twice in the shower, and grabbed my black polyester dress. After a brief shimmy, I yanked the comb through my hair. I applied makeup and tried to send positive thoughts toward the dark bags under my eyes. Then, I began to dig in my suitcase for my black tights. Nothing. I was standing barelegged in my vintage hotel room without tights and without copies—with an impending breakfast interview in forty-five minutes. Did I mention that it was now snowing? Sparkles began to appear in my peripheral vision as I settled into pure panic mode. This was bad. Very bad. With a deep breath, I headed outside to solve my dilemma. I drove back to Super Walmart. The customer service desk was still dark. The sign said that it would not open for an hour.

Fine then, I would solve my hosiery issue first. I had to cover my (slightly) furry legs. I raced to "Ladies Stockings." There, I found an empty shelf. I instantly began to hyperventilate. I scanned frantically and then spotted one small peg with three pairs of black tights near the floor. I reached for a pair and audibly thanked the universe. Then, I paused. The universe responded with a kick in the teeth: a red, prominently printed "QT" was emblazoned across the cardboard package. It quickly became apparent that the only size available was queen size, extra-tall. And, though I had been eating quite a bit of chocolate frosting, I had only reached plump princess size, average height, at best.

Beggars can't be choosers. I grimly headed toward the register. I paid for the tights and stepped into the restroom. I flicked on a dim fluorescent light that buzzed ever so slightly. As I ripped off the packaging, I gasped. The tights were ominously huge. The legs seemed to uncoil for miles, and the elastic waistline was as long as my arm. Remaining determined, I stepped into them. I then pulled the fabric up as far as my underarms. Then, I tucked it under my bra to keep it in place. The stretchy tubes still swam at my ankles and bunched at the knees, but I was covered. Good enough. Thirty minutes to go.

I emerged from the restroom and asked the next employee where I could find a copy machine. Her answer? The local grocery store that was located five miles away. Breathlessly thanking her—and hitching up my new tights, again I ran. After a hasty reprogramming and brief argument with Samantha, I was led down a series of desolate roads. I jumped out of the car with my printout in one hand and my falling waistband in the other. It was there that I found the only publicly available copy machine in this town. It was situated next to the lottery counter and a small dinette that presently hosted a number of locals, drinking coffee and sharing gossip.

As I walked in with my rumpled dress and my tights in a pronounced pool at my feet, I felt their heads turn. Simultaneously, they seemed to give me a once over. I stood there catching my breath, with flushed cheeks and flyaway hair. From their expressions, I could tell the assessment wasn't favorable. I swear that I heard one person mutter, "I don't think she's from here." Others looked down at their coffee, as if embarrassed for me. In response, I gave my newfound audience a weak smile. Then, I turned and inspected the ancient copy machine. I laughed like a crazy person. It was immediately clear that I was in desperate need of a roll of quarters.

The next minutes were a blur of excruciatingly slow copying while I prayed that my tights would not fall completely to the floor for all to see. In the end, I actually made it to my breakfast interview with two minutes to spare. As I gratefully slid into a diner booth and introduced myself, I immediately noticed two things: the faculty interviewer was wearing a cat sweater and also had pronounced bed head. My confidence surged. I inhaled the thick coffee that appeared in a mug on the table. My eyes stung and my throat burned. I was ready. I answered the first question. When the faculty interviewer nodded in agreement, I smiled and leaned back against the slightly sticky, faux-leather seat. No matter how the rest of the day went, I felt victorious: there were still-warm copies in my handbag. That was all that mattered.

I am not ashamed to say that the rest of the day was a success. My presentations were well received, and in my punchy, sleep-deprived state, everyone seemed to find me relatively amusing. I felt an immediate kinship with a few of the faculty members. I even disclosed my hosiery secret to a certain kindred spirit. Her reply? A wink and returned whisper: "They look like Banana Republic to me."

The next day, I was offered the job. Unfortunately, the remote location offered little opportunity for dual employment, so I turned it down. Over the months, Jason and I tried many approaches to find jobs for both of us, but with the sudden shift in the economy, it became an impossibility. We actually had several friends who delayed their doctoral defenses in the hope that the failing economy might be a blip. We soon found that it wasn't. Ultimately we followed a faculty position for Jason in Washington State in a town that, gratefully, contained more than a Super Walmart.

NOTES

1. Not recommended as an option to a dissertation chapter.
2. Do they still say "hip"?
3. This happened more than once.

4

CHANGING CLOTHES IN THE PHONE BOOTH

Jessalynn Strauss

Most people have an identity crisis around midlife where they ask deep-seated and somewhat jarring questions such as, "Who am I, really?" and "What makes me who I am?" I had my own crisis at age 33 when I finished my PhD at a laid-back university in the Pacific Northwest and started teaching as an assistant professor at a private, Catholic university on the border of the Midwest and the South. The adjustment was not an easy one, in no small part because I felt ill equipped to step into a profession—the professoriate—in which I had absolutely no prior work experience. Sure, I'd worked as a professional in my field—public relations and communication—for about six years, about average for those teaching in my discipline. But I was still nervous, even about the little things. How would I convince the students that they should take me seriously? What should I wear? What should I have the students call me?

Whether intentionally or not, I found myself creating a sort of superhero-like alter ego to bolster my confidence. In doing so, I particularly fixated on the latter question, as I thought it was important that an academic superhero have an appropriate moniker. In graduate school, I had students call me by my full name, which seemed appropriately formal since I'd gone by a nickname for most of my life. But although I loved the prospect of being "Dr. Strauss" (in fact, I even had my credit cards reissued to "Dr. Jessalynn Strauss"—don't judge), it seemed overly formal, even for a professor at a private liberal arts university. Eventually, though, I went with "Dr. Strauss," believing that the formality might help establish my credibility. As someone new to the university, and—I really did think this at the time—not terribly older than my students, I felt that I needed the authority of the title. And so Dr. Strauss was born.

It took a while to assimilate the alternate identity that I'd created for myself. As I designed her, Dr. Strauss is the ideal college professor—or, at least, she's my perception of what that ideal should be. Over time, I've developed the different aspects of Dr. Strauss—appearance, behavior, and beliefs—and although it sounds a little crazy, doing so has helped guide my actions through these often-turbulent early years of my teaching career.

A SUPERHERO'S COSTUME

All great superheroes look the part, and because I teach public relations, I understand the importance of perception and first impressions. So I spent hours at low-end department stores (I do have student loans to pay off, after all) trying to put together a professorial wardrobe that would both impress and intimidate the students in my classes. I went shopping at Nordstrom Rack nearly a dozen times, flipping helplessly through racks of pantsuits and trying desperately to cobble together a professional wardrobe. I tried on clothes that were totally out of character for me, but that was the point: I was building an altogether *new* character.

I imagined that I had to live up to a superhero's appearance, and in academia, I imagined that superhero would wear a pencil skirt, tailored shirt, pantyhose, and ballet flats. This was how I had hoped to come across to my students—professional, put-together, and authoritative. But I had trouble keeping up appearances, and over the next few semesters, my standards of attire slowly slipped. I started wearing jeans to teach class, at first only on Fridays, and then on any day with bad weather. I struggled mightily to look the part of a college professor, or at least what I thought that professor should look like.

Eventually I realized that Dr. Strauss was naturally going to look different from the typical academic superhero, because Dr. Strauss *was* different. In fact, being different was one of her strengths. For example, in one class a student submitted a heartfelt essay about how she had come out as a lesbian in the past year. It was on a final exam, and she certainly didn't have to bring up the topic, but she did. I was in tears reading it. I'm not sure if I was more touched at her words or at the fact that she felt comfortable enough with me to share something that couldn't have been easy to discuss, especially at a Catholic university. I think that my willingness to be different had something to do with this student's trust in me.

A SUPERHERO'S TRIALS

While it's important that students feel like they can relate to Dr. Strauss, it's also important they know that they can't walk all over her. In fact, Dr. Strauss is more of a classic old-school college professor: a bit gruff and somewhat feared but ultimately respected. "You have to take Dr. Strauss's class—you'll do a lot of work, but you'll learn a lot, too." "Dr. Strauss's class was the hardest class I've taken, but it was great." "Oh, you have Dr. Strauss next term? She's tough."

Dr. Strauss asks a lot of students, but she gives a lot of herself in return, whether it's encouraging a faltering student in a public speaking class or taking extra time to do an independent study with an exceptional one. As much as I'd like to think that my workday ends at 5:00 p.m. or that my contract runs only nine months, it doesn't. If I want to be good in my job, it can't.

All of this often leads to Dr. Strauss feeling just a bit overworked and put-upon at times. It doesn't help that everyone around me seems to have a perception of what I "do" that isn't grounded in reality. A lot of times, I wish I had the job that my family and nonacademic friends imagine me having: a three-month life of leisure in the summers, and during the school year, a slow-paced workweek where I occasionally pop into a classroom to lecture or grade the odd paper or two. There's often nothing in that picture about the countless meetings I attend, the recommendation letters I write (sometimes for students who only barely deserve it), and the panicked efforts to submit a paper at 11:59 p.m. for a midnight conference deadline, only to find that the site has crashed and my past week's worth of frenzied writing will have to wait for a later conference.

I often wonder what my students think that I "do," although I never ask. Perhaps I'm afraid that the answer is that they don't think about it—much of their actions would tend to indicate this. I'm also afraid that they'll answer, as I suspect they might, that they perceive my duties to be as follows:

- answer any questions they might have on *their* time frame and in a prompt and speedy manner;
- provide, through my in-class lectures, a downtime of fifty or seventy-five minutes where they can check Facebook, text their friends, or do homework for another class while they have a respite from their busy lives of extracurriculars and work obligations;
- deliver said lecture with the technological acuity of a Silicon Valley software whiz, the vocal clarity of a classically trained actor, and the energy of a ten-year-old child;
- give detailed and thorough feedback on their assignments, while ultimately deciding to overlook their numerous errors and give them a grade of A; and, finally,
- write glowing recommendation letters for them in spite of the fact that they only sometimes come to classes, rarely contribute to the classroom environment, and seldom excel in their written assignments.

I realize that I am overly cynical when it comes to my students and their intentions. This has actually been one of my greatest challenges to overcome, because Dr. Strauss is *not* cynical; in fact, she is optimistic and believes that there is good in anyone, just short of being unconscionably gullible or naive. This sometimes leads her to err. Perhaps she might think it not unlikely that five grandmothers have died in a class of seventy-five in the span of a week. She may also find it wholly possible that massive thunderstorms have just happened to cut the power to a student's computer at just the moment that said student was uploading an assignment for an online course, damaging the file irrevocably.

But cynicism can be blinding, and Dr. Strauss has to work hard to find the good in all students. When in the middle of a bitch-fest with fellow professors about this or that student, she must remember that such conversations relieve stress, but they are ultimately unproductive. And while Dr. Strauss might be just as gleefully snarky as Jessalynn, especially when students' behavior is practically begging to be mocked—and so often, they are begging to be mocked!—she won't let it get in the way of doing her job and being an exceptional teacher.

A SUPERHERO'S TRIUMPH

I am widely known in my family as the crazy left-wing liberal college professor, posting political messages on Facebook and—often against my better judgment—engaging in arguments about politics both on- and off-line. So one May afternoon in my second year, I took a break from working and checked my Twitter feed—isn't this the contemporary equivalent of procrastinating by checking one's e-mail?—and found a new video message from an activist group I'd recently joined. The Campaign for Southern Equality challenges unfair marriage laws in the South by supporting same-sex couples that apply for marriage licenses knowing they'll be turned down. I found the coverage of their events—video and print—powerful in a way I can't describe, watching over and over as couples were told they weren't allowed to marry the person they loved. The video message brought me to tears, and as I dunked a tea bag into a cup of hot water, I had a flurry of thoughts. *Everyone needs to see this*, I thought, and moved my cursor over the "Retweet" button. *I should add a comment, to make it clear that I show my support.*

And then I stopped. As someone who teaches public relations, I use my Twitter account to connect with students for teaching purposes. I consider it my "public" social network, whereas private comments (often frustrations about students and the like) are relegated to Facebook. And considering that I was working—as an untenured assistant professor—at a Jesuit Catholic university, to say that I had reason to be concerned about making a public statement about marriage equality would be an understatement. So I asked myself, *What would Dr. Strauss do?* The answer came quickly, and the clarity was a relief. I retweeted the message with an added word of support: "Big supporter of this org. RT @CSElive New WE DO Video about our actions across #NC! Please help us spread the word!"

About an hour later, my phone set off its telltale "ding," alerting me that I'd been mentioned on Twitter. I picked up the phone and unknowingly held my breath while I loaded the app that read my Twitter feed. I switched to the section where it shows tweets where I'd been mentioned and noticed that one of my former students had re-tweeted my message of support for the Campaign for Southern Equality. I exhaled. Certainly, I understand that I can't "convert" my students who might disagree with me on this and other topics. That's not my job, nor is it my right to do so. But as their professor, and their partner in this learning adventure that they're on, I wouldn't be doing them justice if I didn't let them know that I have beliefs and opinions, too.

And more to the point, keeping quiet isn't something Dr. Strauss would do. As I continually face the challenge of doing my job as best I can, it's reassuring to know that I'm acting in a manner that's consistent with my beliefs. While I realize that my political affiliations might not always win me supporters among the students, I also believe that I can't abandon my beliefs altogether in the classroom. Put simply, Dr. Strauss is not an apolitical robot. In fact, I believe that it is her passion about political issues, and the fact that she finds it important to be involved as a citizen, that makes her such a good role model for her students. Sure, she'll make some mistakes—and perhaps being so politically outspoken in this chapter is one of them—but she'll always act according to her moral compass. At the end of the day, that's something she—and I—can live with.

II

Occupational Dissonance

At the top of the list of *things they don't tell you in graduate school* is what the daily life of a professor really looks like. Perhaps you recall walking by professors' offices, some with the doors open, seeming to welcome the errant student to pop in and chat, and others with closed doors but light seeping out from below the doorjamb, the furious sounds of fingers clicking on a keyboard emanating from within. Still others seemed to be departmental phantoms, with marked offices and mailboxes indicating their existence and affiliation with the university but apparating only to teach or attend essential faculty meetings (they all had tenure, of course). Presumably they were writing, grading papers, or getting ready for class, but did you ever think, "What are they actually *doing* in there? What is a professor's working life actually like?"

Recently, one of us (Erin) attended a symposium where scientists were sharing with practicing teachers what they did in their daily work. The first scientist talked about conducting experiments and analyzing data—nothing unexpected. Then the second scientist stood up, put a hand on her hip, and said, "Let me tell you what my day looks like. I go to work, I put on a white lab coat. My computer is in a cubby. I start my day by checking e-mail, and then I have organizational meetings with people that work for me." She went on, accounting for what her "actual" work life looked like—and it involved a lot of drudgery and not a lot of glamour.

A professor's work life is strikingly similar in its drudgery-to-glamour ratio. We spend a lot of time on e-mail, meeting with people, preparing for class, teaching, and writing when we can. Ideally, a professor's daily work is a combination of research, teaching, and service. Depending on the type of university where you work, or the type of position you have, it might be a forty–forty–twenty split, or a twenty–sixty–twenty split, or some other combination. Although, as many have documented, it can easily become all teaching, some mixture of dealing with needy students, putting together the perfect slide show, and slogging through dozens—if not hundreds—of tests or papers. Teaching can quickly become a time suck.

At the same time you're needed (or required to be) elsewhere as a servant of the institution. If you're a go-getter, you might volunteer to be on a lot of committees. If you're a squeaky wheel, you might end up in charge of something because you complained. Or if you're a member of an underrepresented group (i.e., a woman or faculty member of color), you might be assigned to an unfair portion of committees to satisfy diversity requirements.[1] As a consequence of these many demands, research and writing—the metrics by which most tenure cases are determined—get squeezed out.[2]

Unfortunately, failure or success at earning tenure is usually judged by how well we are able to squeeze in actual thinking, research, and writing time into days that are otherwise jam-packed with other commitments over which we have little (or sometimes no) control. The result is dissonance between how we actually spend our time (service and teaching) as compared to how we ultimately will be evaluated (research and writing).

As the chapters in this section indicate, keeping teaching under control can present unforeseen challenges, and the publication process can bedevil even those making the most copious efforts to write. For those of us who are eager do-gooders, the service aspects of our job may lead in unexpected directions (and serve unintended purposes). So here it is, in its unadorned glory: the teaching, research, and service of professors.

NOTES

1. For more on this troubling phenomenon, see Stephen R. Porter, "A Closer Look at Faculty Service: What Affects Participation on Committees?" *Journal of Higher Education* 78, no. 5 (2007): 523–41.

2. This difficulty is taken up and addressed effectively by Paul Silvia in his book *How to Write a Lot: A Practical Guide to Productive Academic Writing* (Washington, DC: American Psychological Association, 2007).

5

WHOSE CLASS IS IT ANYWAY?

Julie C. Mitchell

Recently, Adam Mansbach wrote a "fake college syllabus" for *Salon* that was quite amusing to anyone who has ever taught at a university.[1] He voiced many things that many professors probably don't have the nerve to say. It seems I have plenty of nerve, since this looked an awful lot like my fall syllabus. In addition to the "don't mess with me children" attitude, I gave them a quiz on it. One of the questions was multiple choice with only one answer: NO. Some students found this quite funny, while others were not amused. The least amused student turned out to be the flaky one who failed the course. I'm sure this is entirely coincidental. However, the rest of the students avoided driving me nuts for the entire semester, so I'll totally do this again.

MATHEMATICAL METHODS FOR STRUCTURAL BIOLOGY

Fall 2012
Julie C. Mitchell

Description

The course gives a broad survey of molecular modeling along with numerical and computational tools for practical applications. Given the diverse nature of the students taking the course, and the range of topics from elementary to advanced, most will find both known and new topics among the course materials. The ultimate goal of the course is to expose students to practical working knowledge in the field of computational structural biology, with which they will undertake readings in the past and current literature and complete a project of their choosing.

Prerequisites

This course is intended for advanced undergraduate students or beginning graduate students from mathematics, biochemistry, and biophysics. The minimal prerequisite is mathematical background through vector calculus, though additional math background is helpful. Those enrolling in the math version of the course should have some CS background, whereas this is waived for those enrolling in the biochem version. I will do my best to ensure that everyone finds the material both accessible and challenging.

Grading

Homework	30%	Five Python-based assignments
Quizzes	30%	About one quiz/chapter
Final project	40%	Class project w/presentation

Textbooks

Julie C. Mitchell, "Mathematical Methods for Structural Biology." These free course notes will be distributed via the Learn@UW website. I wrote the notes by copying things off Wikipedia during my sabbatical in Rio when I was not lying on the beach. Accordingly, there may be some leftover spelling errors or caipirinha stains on the pages. Corrections are appreciated.

Course Project

The course project will consist of a computational study on which both a short report and an oral presentation will be given. Students are encouraged to choose projects that are related to their thesis work or future career goals. Students who have neither thesis work nor career goals are welcome to consult with me for ideas.

The oral reports will be presented during the final three lecture periods of the class. Times are assigned randomly but for some reason always seem to correlate with your attendance records. Attendance at all three student-presentation periods is 100 percent mandatory, and failure to attend other students' presentations will result in a reduction of your grade.

Homework and Quizzes

There will be several quizzes on the lecture and reading material, which will be online. There will also be five homework assignments consisting of Python-based modeling exercises. You will need a computer and to install Python, Numerical Python, and Scientific Python on it. I will set some times for people to come in with help on installing on Macs and PCs. Since I don't have a machine running Windows 92, or whatever tricked-out gaming box you use to shoot the enemy on, I can't guarantee the TAs and I will be able to fix all your problems. If you are running Linux, you presumably know enough to not need our help.

I will make some drop-in facilities available to students who can't get this to work on their machines. Help will be available during certain hours. During other hours when people are trying to get their own research and course work done, asking them for help will result in revocation of your drop-in privileges, because I have no incentive to be nice and let you work on our lab computers in that case.

Class Policy

Your attention in class, including not talking, eating loud snack foods, or banging on keyboards, is not only appreciated but also expected. You will be asked nicely not to do this the first time and asked not so nicely the second time; the third time you will be asked to leave class, and the fourth time you will be made to finish the lecture while I click click click my pen and snd txt msgs 2 my bff about ur grade.

Late homework used to be disallowed entirely, but I've gotten nicer in my old age. If you need to turn it in late, you can have a one-week extension, but it costs you 50 percent credit on the assignment. No exceptions to this will be made unless your entire family dies in a freak accident (and you can prove it). Note that early homework is always gladly accepted and is generally the better way to deal with coinciding deadlines.

I enjoy teaching as a function of student interest, so paying attention and asking questions are appreciated. Lest you worry I will make you feel stupid (I have no idea why you might think that), I will actually go out of my way to make your most idiotic question sound like an insightful inquiry, or at least not dumb, because I can often understand why you asked it. It's when you are not respectful of me, those helping with the course, or other students that I will make you feel like an idiot, just so we are clear.

If you are a model student and think I'm being disrespectful to you in the way I'm writing this, you need to laugh more, and you've clearly never taught at a public university. You're getting a PhD, though, so perhaps your turn is coming!

Contact Information

Below is contact information for the professor, postdoc, and graduate student for the course, along with drop-in hours for working on homework and hours during which you can ask designated people for help with it.

Requests for appointments with Professor Mitchell are by e-mail to Professor Mitchell and start with "Dear Professor Mitchell" followed by some semblance of grammar and logic, along with some possible times (meaning more than one) that you hope may be convenient for me. I am generally not available TH before 11:00 a.m., or any other day before 9:00 a.m. After 5:00 p.m., I will be happy to show up to your house with beer and pizza while I personally do all your homework for you the night before it is due. It's true; try asking.

Quotations of the Day

> Sarcasm: it beats killing people.
> —Unknown

> If you think your teacher is tough, wait until you get a boss. (S)he doesn't have tenure.
> —Bill Gates

> For every person who wants to teach there are approximately thirty people who don't want to learn much.
> —W. C. Stellar

Things You Might Learn in This Course If You Pay Attention

The course covers a large range of topics from many STEM fields in a fairly accessible manner. Occasionally, students have commented that they wanted greater depth in some subject, but the problem is that this is different for each student, and thus I'd get a different comment if I changed things. Therefore, I have opted to keep the smorgasbord format.

Many of the subjects below require a course unto themselves to teach in full detail. The point of this course is to expose you to a lot of interesting things that you may need later and get you to apply one of them in detail. I once had a student tell me this was the only course where he ever learned anything he ended up actually using later, by the way.

NOTE

1. Adam Mansbach, "My Fake College Syllabus," *Salon*, January 25, 2013, http://www.salon.com/2013/01/26/my_fake_college_syllabus.

6

WHEN HOMER SIMPSON WRITES HOMER'S *ILIAD*

Preventing Plagiarism while Keeping Your Promotion

Troy Appling

Many of my colleagues know that plagiarism is my "berserk button," something I willingly confess and attribute to occupational hazard as a composition and literature instructor. I also admit that during my early days as a teaching assistant and then adjunct instructor, I was more than willing to advocate branding a scarlet *P* on offending students. Later, as a newly minted PhD in literature, I was thrilled to be offered a tenure-track position at a local two-year state college teaching the usual composition-plus-literature-survey-plus-occasional-special-topics load.

Within one semester, though, I quickly discovered that the strictures of integrity that I had considered sacrosanct in my own academic pursuits were a lot more fluid in the minds of my students. One budding young scholar once told me that he thought MLA citation was pointless, since if you really wanted to know where he got the information, you could "Google it," just as he did. Besides, he was going to be a nurse and wouldn't need to know how to cite Shakespeare in "the real world."

After about a half dozen plagiarism convictions ranging from improper paraphrasing and citation to using the ComposeMyEssay.com–style cut-and-paste method, I finally decided that merely venting at my colleagues over lunch after giving zeros was not enough. A quick flip through some of my plagiarism "case files" is enough to illustrate the dilemma.

EXHIBIT A

During my first semester teaching on the college level, as a teaching assistant fresh out of training from the University of Memphis and Florida State University, I had a particular student who struggled unsuccessfully all semester to compose a college-level paper. He consistently ended up with C or D papers, no matter how much extra time he spent in my office and in the Reading/Writing Center. Furthermore, this young sage was quite open about his opinion of the course—he was bored and reminded me on a couple of occasions that he was only there because the class was required for his major.

His passion, or at least his passionate surliness, did not translate into his writing, however. All semester long his papers were filled with choppy ramblings, with nary a semicolon or complex sentence in sight. Thus when it came time to submit his final essay—an argumentative research paper—I was shocked. The first sentence was a jaw-dropping fourteen-word compound-complex sentence, one of those pieces of beauty that brings composition teachers to their knees in tearful joy, as all good and rare artworks should.

Yet I always warn my students on the first day that anyone who spends all semester writing Homer Simpson yet suddenly turns in Homer's *Iliad* for a final paper raises a warning flag. Thus, after a brief moment of *Wow! My scintillating pedagogy hath brought forth a new voice into the cosmos*, reality set in, and I continued to read not with a sense of accomplishment but with cynical suspicion.

Chagrined, I performed the required digital due diligence through web searches and plagiarism-detection software. (On a side note, why don't our students believe us when we tell them that we can Google just as well as they can?) Surprise of surprises, I discovered that not only did that first sentence come from another source but also so did all the other sentences—nine pages worth! The student had spent about fifty dollars at a "paper mill" website in order to avoid doing the work himself.

The Sentence

The first-year writing program had very strict procedures, so I bounced it up the jurisdictional chain, along with my highlighted printouts, screen shots, and recommendations for tarring and feathering. The student had to appear before the department's director of undergraduate studies and was forced to accept a zero for the course. All was right with the world.

Yet the story does not end there. A few weeks after the semester ended, I got an e-mail from the student. At first I thought it was some sort of apology but far from it. In fact, the student was asking me to help him get his money back from the paper mill, since they had apparently guaranteed that he would not get caught. (I believe this is a classic example of "chutzpah.") Needless to say, I declined to assist and never did find out if he was successful in his pursuit.

EXHIBIT B

A few years later, one of my online composition students did not follow the instructions requiring that she submit her final draft as an attached file in the drop box of our learning management system. Instead, she pasted her fifteen-hundred-word treatise into the comment box—without removing any of the blue-underlined hyperlinks. The hyperlinks took me directly to Wikipedia.

The Sentence

Failure of assignment. At least she made my job of highlighting the plagiarized sections much easier.

EXHIBIT C

This past semester my online freshmen had to write what I call their "Passion Paper," where they argue a thesis about either a professional passion (their major or occupation) or a social issue about which they feel strongly. One of my dual-enrolled high schoolers, a sophomore in his first college class, submitted as his opening sentences something along the lines of, "In my twenty years of life, I have struggled to find love. Now that I have a boyfriend, though, things are much different."

You can see where I might have been a bit suspicious that this was not his original work, especially considering that his biographical post on the first day of class included details about his age and school grade, as well as a picture of him and his girlfriend. Sure enough, a quick web search revealed an almost-decade-old blog post from an Asian college student living in Australia.

The Sentence

Failure of assignment.

EXHIBIT D (MY PERSONAL FAVORITE)

Stupidity, unfortunately, is still not a crime, either inside or outside the ivory tower. I was teaching an upper-level contemporary drama course as a teaching assistant at Florida State and required the students to write a mini-biography and analysis of a playwright chosen from a list I provided.

As I was reading through the final submissions, I came across one that seemed to really comprehend the assignment and that provided a level of insight that was regretfully lacking in many of the other papers. The further I read, though, the stronger my sense of déjà vu became. After the second page or so, it finally dawned on me why this particular analysis seemed so familiar. It should have; after all, I was the one who had originally written it the year before.

The student had copied approximately one thousand words from an article that I had had published, never once making the connection between my name and the name on the source text. I had even referenced the essay in class. It was, after all, my first peer-reviewed publication.

The Sentence

Failure of the course. (It should be noted that the draconian sentence levied here was not proportionally derived from the idiocy involved but because it was not the student's first offense.)

DEFENSE 1: I'VE GOT BETTER THINGS TO DO, BECAUSE LIFE IS TOUGH

Whenever I catch a plagiarist, I almost invariably hear one of four defenses. The first comes from the most blatant and belligerent students, who will time and again argue that a self-reflective five-page essay was not as important as other priorities in the grand scheme of their well-thought-out lives; besides, they note, they figured that they would not get caught anyway. The more brazen ones can even become offended at the accusation of wrongdoing, suggesting that it is somehow the professor's fault that the student was forced to resort to such reprehensible behavior. The syllabus made me do it?

I understand that life gets in the way and that sometimes education has to take a backseat to economics. Most of us have experienced those "semesters of the apocalypse" where Murphy and his law seemed to trample gleefully over our academic plans. My semester of the apocalypse was spring of my junior year when, in between taking eighteen hours of upper-division humanities and literature courses, working in the campus computer lab, and interning at a job off campus, I managed to sneak in a car wreck, a dislocated shoulder, two deaths (not my own), and the hospitalization of three family members. It's not my fault; my advisor told me that extracurricular activities looked good on graduate school applications. I guess he should have been more specific.

Yet not once during this tumultuous time did I consider plagiarism or any other form of cheating. Instead I went to my professors and explained the situation, asking for a project extension in one case and an assignment modification in another. Surprisingly enough, none of these kindly scholars morphed into fierce unholy beasts determined to disintegrate my troubled undergraduate self and devour my scholastic soul. They reacted in compassion, helping me to succeed with a 4.0 that semester in spite of all the distractions, and I would like to think that I am able to return the favor to my students now.

This is one of the reasons we as scholars do what we do. We are attempting to compassionately educate our students and model the tenets of academic integrity, regardless of hardship or distraction, whether personal or professional.

DEFENSE 2: WHAT? WIKIPEDIA ISN'T COMMON KNOWLEDGE?

The next defense often takes the form of, "I thought that if I changed a few words here or there, it wasn't plagiarism." If I had a dollar for every time I've heard that, I would almost certainly be done paying off my student loans by now. Students often come to us woefully uneducated about what defines appropriate scholarship on the college level. This is not to say that public school teachers are doing a poor job. On the contrary, since their focus by definition has to be more broadly based, they do not have the time to devote to the intricacies of MLA formatting, or the proper procedures for creating a double-blind experiment.

Where I teach, we have determined that students often need training not only on how to cite and incorporate sources but also on how to evaluate them in the first place. Wikipedia, for example, has its uses as an initial source or springboard, despite the fact that one of my students told me that her high school English teacher would call me a heretic for suggesting this. However, I encourage my students to immediately branch out into more scholarly directions, a concept that often baffles them. Many of them seem to operate on the assumption that if it is on the Internet it must be true, at which point I ask them if they have ever seen something false posted on a social networking site.

As a younger professor—let's temporarily ignore my recent epiphany that I am now twice as old as some of my students—I like many in my station find myself in a curiously liminal position, acting as both liaison and interpreter. On the one hand, there is the established faculty, whose hard work and years of discipline have instilled in them a deep respect for the effort that good scholarship entails. On the other hand, you have students, especially first-time collegians, who have grown up in a world of instant gratification, entitlement, the Internet, and "What the heck is microfiche?"

Even if they do not understand the complex arbitrariness of varying citation styles, something those of us in school for decades—admit it—still struggle with, most students at least grasp the concept of using quotation marks around direct quotes. However, this is only a small step in the right direction. We have to teach our students what to do after the quote is inserted, after the data is collected, and after the equations are presented. We have to teach them how to add to those examples in such a way as to bolster an argument or prove a hypothesis.

We "whippersnappers," as one of my former mentors called those of us on annual contract, are often more closely linked with these digital natives, especially in lower-division courses, and it falls to us to educate them not only on the definitions and examples of academic honesty but also on why such behavior is necessary. We stress the importance of "How does this help humanity?" in a world increasingly overrun with "How does this help my GPA?" and "How do I even start this thing?"

DEFENSE 3: YOU WANT ME TO DO WHAT, EXACTLY?

Those of us brand new to the tenure track are no doubt quite familiar with the vagaries of professional academic life. Life as a teaching assistant or adjunct in some ways was comparatively blissful, at least academically if not financially; you focused on sticking to the syllabus and interacting with your students on a regular basis. While that still happens as a full-time academic, other layers of fun and festivity compound the complexity.

Thus, it is easy for me to relate to the third defense I hear from cheaters: "I did not understand the assignment." Ironically, it is precisely because they did not grasp the instructions that I am able to catch some of the more subtle offenders. They find an essay that seems close, such as one about the same story or author. Then they change a word here or there and fire it off to the digital drop box in hopes that their duplicity will slip by unnoticed in the 8.2 million other papers that I have to grade that week.

What they fail to realize is that I, like many professors, specifically tailor my assignments to synthesize specific elements and course objectives, making it difficult to just pull something off of an Internet shelf and turn it in. I had one student tell me, "I don't understand why you gave me a D on this assignment. I failed this class last semester with Professor So-and-So, but she gave me a B for this same essay." Maybe so, but (a) I'm not that professor, and (b) her assignment was looking for something different than mine even though they were both about Ernest Hemingway or William Shakespeare or whatever.

As part of the opening-day lecture of any of my classes, I tell my newcomers that I have three degrees—one in humanities and the other two in English. I am a published writer, and I even like to read books for fun. This means a couple of things. First of all, I have student loans. Second, yes, I am a professional nerd. I came to terms with these facts a long time ago and have accepted them gracefully, at least the nerd part. Third, these degrees also mean that in the field of literature and writing I have a little knowledge and that I know what I am doing.

However, I stress to the class that I am not to be put up on a pedestal. One side effect of my nerdiness is that sometimes what makes perfect sense to me in an assignment instruction sheet will not translate well into the real world. I try to emphasize to my students that while I do take the course seriously, and that they will rigorously engage the course materials throughout the semester, I would like to think that I am not a bespectacled scholarly version of Dr. Evil. I am not secretly plotting to destroy their college and career aspirations by assigning them incomprehensible and mind-numbing assignments hopelessly beyond their understanding. I point out from the beginning, even before I assign the first paragraph, that they can and should come talk to me at the first sign of confusion.

Perhaps it is because I am new to the profession. After all, I know of some senior faculty at other institutions who take the baby bird approach to assignments. They toss the student out of the scholarly nest, so to speak, with nothing but an instruction sheet, and it is up to the student to either take flight or crash in a failing heap; the professor won't be there either way except to evaluate the results. Yet, I believe that good professors should offer specific guidance and advice, not cryptic fortune-cookie riddles, which should be saved for faculty mixers, the annual Christmas banquet, or annotations of your graduate student's thesis notes.

To minimize confusion in our courses, many of my colleagues and I focus on the process, especially with composition assignments. Consider a typical essay for my Freshman Composition class, which usually takes about four weeks to complete. The same day that I assign the topic, I require my students to submit a brainstorming list at the end of the period, a prospectus of sorts that lets me know that they understand the concept and direction of the paper, even if they have not chosen a specific topic. Within two weeks, I have them turn in a rough draft to me, and also to a workshop group of their peers, which offers confused students another outlet to seek clarity, since they often feel more comfortable asking their peers for advice rather than coming to me directly.

DEFENSE 4: I NEED TO LEARN TIME TRAVEL AND LEARN IT YESTERDAY!

By far the most common rationale for academic dishonesty is time constraints. "I ran out of time"; "I got too busy at work/home/other classes/CIA missions to Moscow"; or, my favorite, "Five pages is way too much for you to expect us to write in only three weeks." Because they often do not know how to plan properly, students find themselves under the looming specter of a deadline, without any idea of how to proceed. Since they are digital natives, much of whose culture centers on media and the Internet, they frequently turn to the web for quick solutions, sometimes at the expense of their ethical integrity.

These are the students, remember, whose first line of intellectual inquiry almost always comes in a browser. During my annual lecture on the importance of definitions in composition, for instance, when I ask how they determine the meaning of an unknown word while reading a textbook, the unanimous first response without fail is "Google it" or "dictionary.com," followed distantly by such expected answers as "context clues," "ask someone else," or the ever-popular "skip it completely."

We untenured professors are frequently still close enough to our graduate school experience to remember panicked late-night writing marathons or weekends sequestered in a locked room with nothing but a glass of water and a spreadsheet of experimental result data. Yet, we have also learned the importance of pacing and breathing room, and how waiting until the last minute is just begging Murphy to show up for a visit.

As I mentioned in the previous point, I break my composition assignments into discrete steps and grade the students on their process as well as their product. In addition to alleviating confusion, such process-based writing forces the students to get in the habit of pacing themselves. Even if they wait to complete the assignment until the night before the rough draft is due, they are still left with a draft, albeit one of less-than-stellar quality, which they will then have at least a week to meditate on and revise.

Although my students balk at it since they have been trained from elementary school to "fire and forget" their essays and often operate under the impression that their essays spring from their heads, Athena-like, in fully formed perfection, most eventually come around to seeing the benefit of this technique. I have also discovered that the process approach cuts down on plagiarism. Since students have a chance to breathe in between drafts, they avoid writer's block and reduce stress, which in turn reduces the likelihood of cheating.

If a student does plagiarize in a draft, I have more responses at my disposal. I use inadvertent offenses as opportunities for remedial instruction (thus sparing my retention rate, by the way). On the other hand, more egregious or flagrant plagiarism still allows me the option of either failing them for the assignment or requiring a complete rewrite on a different topic for a lesser grade (again sparing my batting average).

THE VERDICT

I admit it: my goal is to disassociate. Like most of us chasing the mysterious tenure, with its attendant angel music and appropriate genuflection on the part of adjuncts and graduate students, I want to drop the word "associate" from in front of "professor" on my business cards. If I were at a larger institution, Behemoth University, for instance, I realize that such a promotion would likely require publications galore, laser light shows, and possibly a shift in the space-time continuum. Yet I can assure you that even at my current institution, a two-year college that has just recently started phasing in four-year degrees, tenure is as elusive a carrot as it is among my university-level brethren.

Those blessed souls who have earned their corner offices and distinguished chairs or couches or whatnot are perhaps somewhat insulated from the forces of academic dishonesty such as listed above. They don't deal as frequently with undergraduates (except in lecture halls holding several hundred of them at once); that's what teaching assistants are for, right?

In addition, at many larger schools, the focus is on research or training upper-level majors in a specific discipline. By this point in their careers, these students ought to know better than to plagiarize or otherwise cheat, although I will point out that there is at least one *obviously* reputable website that promises not only to write undergraduate essays for a fee but also to write dissertations as well. No, it is those of us who have not yet reached the educational Elysian fields who most frequently encounter students trying to "pull a fast one."

Yet it is precisely this fact that highlights why we should be concerned about the larger issue of plagiarism and academic integrity. Consider that at many institutions where research is a primary focus, part of the tenure decision is based on demonstration of scholarly and research prowess: publications, grants received, or experimental results achieved, for example. These successes are most often determined by peer review—fellow academics and experts in the field who are qualified to evaluate the subject matter at hand.

While I covet the recognition of my peers in the form of publications, conference presentations, favorable reviews, and of course cash, the placard on my office door will be engraved at the behest of two much larger, more directly involved groups: the administration, and the students themselves.

TENURE IN THE HANDS OF AN ANGRY MOB

For places such as community colleges where research is less of a focus, teaching becomes the touchstone of evaluation. This takes two forms at my college and comes from two different directions. The first component is a pedagogical evaluation, which comes from above: the administration. In my case, the dean or vice president sits in on a class or two once a year and then meets with me to discuss strengths and weaknesses of my in-class techniques, as well as other educational components such as online presence, syllabi, course policies, and communication skills.

Although I have known of some instructors who balk at such observations, considering them to be too intrusive, nerve-wracking, or both, I actually look forward to the feedback and like to think that I have benefitted from each of my performance evaluations. Mr. Vice President for academic programs, please take note.

Yet I mentioned that our evaluations come from two directions. Even the review from above incorporates evaluation from below. I mean, of course, the students—both their end-of-term evaluations and their performance, which is often measured in retention rates. My students are generally positive in their formal evaluations (the occasional "He didn't give me an A" or "He makes us think too much" notwithstanding), but often their success rates reveal a more complex and interesting story. It is clear that in many places a driving factor in evaluations, individually and corporately, is a high number of successful students. I have heard anecdotal evidence at other institutions where a success rate of below 70 percent initiates red alert klaxons, National Guard deployment, and spontaneous combustion—or at least a serious meeting, documented in triplicate, with the chair of the department.

As is often the case with raw statistics, though, the numbers can at times give an inaccurate portrayal of the situation. The data has to account for performance issues beyond the professor's control, such as student withdrawals, financial aid problems, or—to bring this back around to the topic at hand—plagiarism. Note that the cases mentioned at the beginning of this chapter divide neatly into two results: failure of the entire course and failure of the individual assignment.

When I was a teaching assistant under the auspices of Florida State University's first-year writing program, I did not have to worry about tenure concerns or success percentages. My classroom functioned as a pedagogical laboratory, with the understanding that as long as I did not go to extremes with either grade inflation or grade deflation, I was given the guided freedom necessary to hone the basics of my craft. Nor did I have to worry too much about retention rates as a community college adjunct. With seven zillion students in Freshman Comp I and II each semester, there were always sections available for me to teach, as long as I followed the departmental syllabus and met with my faculty mentor once a semester or so. In both cases, any instances of plagiarism were beyond my control in that the consequences were clearly laid out by others higher up the academic ladder. Things became more complex, if not less clear, when I became a full-time academic. At an open-access institution with only three and a half full-time English faculty—we share one professor with the Developmental Studies program—each professor becomes individually responsible for the performance of his or her students and with dealing with plagiarists in our midst.

The first semester I arrived, two students decided to turn in the exact same paper, each one titled "Men and Women Are Different." The essays turned out to be both blatantly obvious and blatantly plagiarized. Upon confrontation with the evidence, each student confessed and apologized, and in both cases it was a first offense. Following the procedure of my previous institutions, I recommended failure for the entire course. After talking things over with my two senior colleagues, though, each of whom has over two decades at the college, I came to realize that our student body needed a different approach. Far from suggesting a mere symbolic punishment, the tenured wisdom recommended having the students fail the assignment yet maintain the possibility of passing the course if they aced each of the remaining course requirements. Although neither faculty member ever mentioned it, I later realized that this course of action not only helped the students learn a valuable lesson about academic integrity and making good choices but also avoided adding an F to my ledger, thus dropping my overall retention rate by almost 10 percent. I began to wonder if some less ethical instructors, or other institutions where the tenure track is more competitive and cutthroat, might let plagiarists slide with a mere tongue lashing if it meant that their batting average would stay in the green.

So how do we balance the need to help students succeed, keep them happy and willing to give us high marks on internal evaluations as well as on professor-rating websites, uphold academic standards, *and* maintain high retention rates that accurately reflect our students' mastery of the material? The first duty is to step back and realize that plagiarists are not the equivalent of scholarly Vikings, pillaging and murdering facts and data in the effort to conquer the mighty Essayland or the Research Project Islands. Nor should they be forced to wear scarlet letters for the rest of their academic careers. If our mission as educators is truly to pass on skills, knowledge, and a passion for our respective disciplines, then the response to academic improprieties such as plagiarism must be proactive rather than reactive. This is especially critical for those of us at teaching-centered organizations.

MOVING BEYOND THE BOILERPLATE

In each of my classes, whether face-to-face or in video lectures for my online students, I speak at length about academic integrity, and specifically about the issue of plagiarism, since it is obviously the most prevalent such issue in a composition classroom. I explain the difference between direct quotations and paraphrasing, and we talk about placing our voices in the chorus of human experience, although I don't usually wax quite so poetically in front of the undergrads. I do have a reputation to uphold, even if it is a nerdy one. I also read the standard "Dear student, don't do this" template language from course policy sheets seen the world over.

My boilerplate language on every syllabus reads,

> Cheating, plagiarism, bribery, misrepresentation, and fabrication are not permitted and will be dealt with severely. Students should make themselves aware of the student code of conduct found in the Student Handbook. You may not purposefully deceive any official of the College by cheating on any assignment, examination, or paper. Cheating is the use of anyone else's work, whether he/she is a student or not, as your own. It is expected that the work you submit in all of your courses is your own. Within the context of this course we will discuss appropriate text citation; incorrect use of outside sources is plagiarism and is academically dishonest. Any academic dishonesty will result in the failure of that assignment as the minimum punishment; it most likely will result in failure of the course and thus may result in dismissal from the college.

I do have to be careful when reading this section, though, after the one time I accidentally slipped midway into a poor imitation of Sam the Eagle, the super-serious basso profundo Muppet with no sense of humor. In my mind this statement seems quite straightforward—here's what academic dishonesty is; don't do it, and if you do, here's what will happen. Game, set, match. My students, if truth be told, often see this information as just another element of a boring legal disclaimer at the beginning of a semester, and they listen mindlessly to the lecture. It is the academic equivalent of clicking "I have read and agree to the license agreement" when installing software on the computer; how often do people read those in their entirety, even though they are legally bound by their contents? Just click yes and get it over with.

Obviously, something is not working; academic dishonesty still occurs, suggesting that a mere definition and consequence list is not enough to educate and deter students from the temptation to cheat. The goal of the academic community at all levels should be to help combat such unethical behavior. My experience with cheating offers some guidance on how to address the issue.

In a perfect world, numbers would not factor into tenure decisions. Regardless of institution, we would all be judged solely on our passion and expertise in our respective disciplines. Of course, in a perfect world, our monthly paychecks would have at least seven digits before the decimal, and essays would be self-grading. Numbers do matter, if only inasmuch as they reflect how well our students have embraced our course material.

Although my background is in in-depth research and literary analysis, I have had to adjust my methods so that even my students whose writing goals only include signing their names on their paychecks will understand that academic honesty, while not a life-or-death matter by any means, is nonetheless an issue worth examining because it makes them better students, better colleagues, and ultimately, better members of society. This civic-mindedness is of course why many of us got into this profession in the first place, why we work so hard for so little and put up with the absurdities of academia.

7

HOW NOT TO TEACH A CLASS

Andrew Shtulman

My first duty as assistant professor at Occidental College was to attend an orientation for new faculty. There we were bestowed with advice from senior faculty, including a history professor who warned us that we ought to keep a box of tissues on hand for the students who get emotional discussing the material. My immediate thought was that the students in a history class might get emotional about racism and genocide, but the students in my classes—Research Methods and Cognitive Psychology—couldn't possibly get emotional about counterbalancing techniques for a repeated-measures design or empirical methods for studying the time course of auditory perception. If those topics bring you to tears, it's tears of boredom not tears of sorrow. Little did I suspect that only three weeks later I would be consoling a weeping student. She wasn't weeping about the material, of course. She was weeping about her grades. Thus began what I now affectionately refer to as my "semester from hell," or "SFH" for short. It was the first semester I taught my own courses, as opposed to assisting someone else, and it was the first semester I discovered that being a teacher requires as thick a skin as being a researcher, if not thicker.

I began the semester expecting that my only real challenge lay in determining what content to teach and how to teach it. But the more significant challenge, I came to realize, was determining what my students expected of me and how to manage those expectations. There's a "strategic" or "tactical" dimension to teaching that no one warns you about or prepares you for, and it's this dimension that caused me the most grief in my SFH.

Some of the errors I made that semester are embarrassingly naive, but I recount them nonetheless in the spirit of full disclosure. I've organized my errors into a set of six big "don'ts": *don't* let students call you by your first name; *don't* be too specific about your grading criteria; *don't* offer to read drafts; *don't* hand back an exam at the beginning of class; *don't* make bargains over grades; and *don't* lose sight of the big picture. Notably missing from this list are any "dos," but that's not an oversight. I simply have no positive advice to offer, and, if I did, who would want to take advice from someone who committed all those don'ts? All I can say is that, since becoming more cognizant of the strategic dimensions of teaching, my semesters have gone from hellish to pleasant, even enjoyable on occasion. I wouldn't yet describe them as "heavenly," but I'm at least at the level of purgatory.

LESSON 1: DON'T LET STUDENTS CALL YOU BY YOUR FIRST NAME

My first challenge came as a complete surprise. I had written a short e-mail to the undergraduates in my Methods class, and as I approached the end, I realized I didn't know how to sign it. As a teaching assistant in graduate school, I had signed all my e-mails "Andrew," but I was a graduate student then and wasn't much worried about the professional distance between my students and me. Graduate students are still *students* after all—older and wiser than undergraduates, perhaps, but students nonetheless. Now I was a *professor*, and I didn't know how *professors* were supposed to sign their e-mails. Professor Shtulman? Dr. Shtulman? Andrew Shtulman, PhD? I decided to go with what was most familiar—"Andrew"—and thus committed a terrible mistake.

Signing my first name only gave the impression that my students and I were on equal footing—that we were colleagues, collaborators, and even chums. Clearly, I wanted my classroom to have a friendly atmosphere and for students to view me as a friendly person, but I didn't intend to suggest a lack of hierarchy. After all, as instructor, I was charged not only with the "friendly" task of imparting knowledge but also with the not-so-friendly task of providing feedback. And when I started to provide that feedback—the kind of honest, critical feedback that any good instructor should provide—I saw an immediate backlash in attitudes and behaviors. Friends don't give friends Ds on their papers, or so I've been told.

Not all students that semester gave me grief over their grades, just some. They were a cast of characters I'll call "Greg," "Peter," "Bobby," "Marcia," "Jan," and "Cindy," for the sake of anonymity. The student I'll call Greg was the most troublesome. "Andrew," he said, popping his head around the door to my office, "I have some questions about my grade on assignment 1." Naturally, I had invited this kind of informality in my e-mail, but I hadn't expected it to spill over into face-to-face interactions. In fact, most students had spontaneously addressed me as "Professor Shtulman" or just "Professor" when they realized they couldn't pronounce "Shtulman." Greg, dissatisfied with his grade on assignment 1, had decided to use the informality of being on first-name terms as a kind of weapon. Calling me "Andrew" to my face was a way of cutting me down to size, a way of questioning my authority. And question my authority he did, raising concerns about my grading criteria ("Why did you take off points here?"), my judgment ("Are you sure you read that paragraph?"), and even my credentials ("Have you ever taught before?"). I wanted to smash Greg's hand in the stapler sitting within arm's reach on my desk, but I politely restrained myself.

From that unpleasant interaction onward, I began to sign all class e-mails "Prof. Shtulman." It's become such an ingrained habit that I occasionally sign "Prof. Shtulman" to family and friends, oddly seeming to brag about my credentials in a communication about travel plans or groceries.

I've noticed that most of my colleagues avoid signing their first names as well. If it's not "Professor X," then it's their initials, their last name, or even nothing at all—odd but effective, I suppose. I do know a few colleagues who actively eschew the formality of titles and insist that their students call them by their first name, but I don't know how they navigate the erosion of professional boundaries this practice invites. My guess is they care more about being perceived as cool and would scoff at anyone who used the phrase "professional boundaries" in a sentence about teaching. But that's the burden we uncool professors have to bear.

Signing "Prof. Shtulman" took care of the "Hey, Andrew" problem immediately. I now make a joke of the whole issue on the first day of class. I ask students to introduce themselves, including both their name and nickname. As an example, I announce, "My name is Andrew Shtulman, and my nickname is Professor Shtulman." I then pause for the laughter that ensues, following it up with "Seriously, if you call me 'Andrew,' I'll break your leg with a steel pipe." Okay, so I only *think* the latter. But, miraculously, I've not had need for steel pipes since my SFH. The precedent I establish on day 1 makes a lasting impression, even among the students whom I eventually come to know very well. I was recently informed by a research assistant that I had (unwittingly) signed an e-mail to another assistant "Andrew," and the recipient was so surprised that he printed it out and circulated it among his peers, bragging that he and I were on first-name terms. While his gesture was a little pathetic, I was flattered nonetheless.

LESSON 2: DON'T BE TOO SPECIFIC ABOUT YOUR GRADING CRITERIA

Grading is the most thankless part of teaching. We spend hours reading uninspired variations of the same basic response, parsing ungrammatical sentences and incomplete thoughts, all to write comments in the margins that typically go unread. Students who do well rarely thank us for our commendations, but students who do poorly are sure to confront us about our criticisms.

None of this occurred to me, however, when I collected my first stack of papers. I was actually elated that students had unquestioningly completed an assignment of my own devising. Holding those papers made me feel like a "real" teacher, like the class had bought into the idea that I was a genuine authority on research methods. Five minutes later, the dread of grading set in as I suddenly realized two things: (1) I had not budgeted enough time for grading into my weekly schedule; and (2) I had not devised a rubric. I was most concerned about the latter, though not for the reasons you might expect.

I wasn't concerned that I had failed to disclose my grading criteria up front. I also wasn't concerned about needing objective criteria to use as *justifications* for my grades—my defense for when the C students came knocking with torches and pitchforks. Rather, I was terrified by the ambiguity of it all. How was I going to separate the A papers from the B papers from C papers? Number of words? Cleverness of title? Choice of font? My mother-in-law suggested I "just give them all As," but that seemed like cheating. I needed to devise a *system*.

The assignment itself was to read two articles—a journal article and a newspaper article reporting on its findings—and assess how well the latter represented the former. I decided that the most efficient way to grade the responses was to first count all the ways that the newspaper article had misrepresented the journal article, and then compare my number to the number that students had identified on their own. I identified a total of six misrepresentations; the students had identified between one and four. My grading woes were thus answered: I'd give the fours an A, the threes a B, the twos a C, and the ones a D, with pluses and minuses thrown in for good measure. The average grade worked out to be a B–, so I was quite satisfied with the result. My satisfaction didn't last long. After class, a parade of students came to see me during office hours, including the student I mentioned earlier who cried over her low grade. Consoling a weeping student was unpleasant, especially without that damned box of tissues I was advised to buy. But even less pleasant was my interaction with a student I'll call Peter.

Peter was, by no small coincidence, a good friend of Greg's. He was bent on challenging *my* interpretation of *his* interpretation of the assignment. Armed with my rubric, he proceeded through it point by point, arguing that he had found all six misrepresentations. He hadn't by any stretch of the imagination, but that didn't stop him from lecturing me on my incompetence as a grader for five whole minutes. I had tuned out after thirty seconds, however, my thoughts turning instead to finger-crushing staplers and leg-crushing pipes.

What that interaction taught me was that, regardless of how carefully I grade, I have to be particularly cautious of my grading criteria. If the criteria are too specific, then they are too vulnerable to retort. One solution I toyed with was abandoning the rubric altogether and slapping a single, holistic assessment at the top (as in, "Sorry, Peter, but this paper sucks: D–"). That's the grading strategy I had encountered most often as an undergraduate (as in, "Wow, Andrew, this paper is amazing: A+"). But it's not a strategy I felt comfortable with as a professor—at least not for papers.

Grading participation, on the other hand, is better as a holistic assessment. The problem is that participation is hard to break down and quantify. During my SFH, I devised what I thought was a simple and objective solution. Everyday I recorded whether each student was absent (coded as a "0" in my grade book), present but comatose (coded as a "1"), or present and responsive (coded as a "2"). My training as a social scientist appears to have cultivated an obsessive need to quantify human behavior, even when teaching. The procedure took a lot of effort, but the payoff was a concrete distribution of scores that I could turn into a concrete measure of participation. In the syllabus, I had warned that "attendance alone is not sufficient to earn a high participation grade; you must actually *participate* if you hope to earn more than a passing grade," and, true to my warning, students who came to class but did not actually say anything—that is, the comatose ones—earned grades in the C range.

Once again, my satisfaction fizzled as students who had earned Cs started e-mailing me about their grades. Apparently, students expect that participation grades are always in the A to B range. As one student, who I'll call Marcia, explained, "I have come across an issue that is very confusing and upsetting to me. I do not see why I have received a 78 in participation, a grade significantly lower than the class average. I feel that to have a grade this much lower than the average I had to have done something counterproductive, or disrupted the class in some way." Marcia had many ones but few twos in my participation log. She consistently came to class but rarely said a word. I responded to Marcia's e-mail by explaining my grading criteria, pointing out that speaking in class is a very modest measure of participation. She responded, "Believe it or not, I did not write to you merely to attempt to gain a change in my grade. I wrote to you because I genuinely do not believe that I was such a significant distance below average in participation and because this calculation seems so subjective I am personally hurt." I was stunned. How could Marcia interpret this blatantly *objective* calculation as *subjective*? And how could she have failed to realize how *below average* her participation had been?

All the work I had put into devising an objective measure of participation was for naught. Students who received low grades, I realized, would be pissed regardless of how objective it was. So after that semester, I abandoned my fancy algorithm and adopted a much simpler procedure: I now assign a participation grade between 80 and 100 based solely on a subjective and retrospective assessment, as I suspect most of my colleagues do. It's less objective than my original measure, but it's *perceived* as more objective, so go figure.

LESSON 3: DON'T OFFER TO READ DRAFTS

About a third of the way into my SFH, Greg and I had another run-in. After receiving "unacceptable" grades on assignments 1 through 3—grades in the B+ to A– range, I should add—Greg decided to take a different tack on assignment 4. This time, he asked if I would review a draft. Though not thrilled by the idea of doing more grading, I couldn't think of any pedagogically sound reason to deny it. It was my job, after all, to help students reach their full potential, and what better way than to provide feedback in the formative stages of their work? Reluctantly, I consented on the provision that he submit his draft at least a week before the final paper was due.

Like clockwork, a draft appeared in my inbox exactly one week before the due date, down to the minute. I thought the early deadline might be prohibitive, but it wasn't to Greg, who seemed hell-bent on getting an A. (Whether he was hell-bent on actually *learning* is another matter.) I opened the draft, made some comments in the margin, and sent it back within the hour. It seemed like an acceptable amount of work for the presumed payoff: a paper from Greg actually worthy of an A and thus a paper he would not bother me about later on.

That payoff was not to come. In the final version, Greg had done virtually nothing to address my concerns. I say *virtually* nothing because he did, in fact, add a couple of words to one paragraph and delete a couple of words from another, but he made no substantive changes to the paper's content or structure. Frustrated by Greg's seemingly willful disregard for my time and effort, I penalized his paper for the unaddressed problems more severely than I penalized other papers containing the same problems but that I had not reviewed earlier. Greg discovered the inequity immediately, having compared his paper to Peter's. He confronted me about it the next day. I explained my reasons for grading his paper more stringently, but he refused to accept them as legitimate. Instead, he repeatedly pointed to the fact that his rough draft and his final draft were not identical, which "obviously" meant that he had heeded my concerns. Greg was also incensed by the discovery that, in reviewing his final paper, I had noticed an additional problem that I had failed to notice in the draft. I was unaware that I had done so, but I was not apologetic when confronted with the news. "That's just the nature of the review process," I explained. "Problems that are overlooked on the first review may very well be discovered on the second."

Greg never submitted another draft to me. In fact, my intransigence on the issue was sufficiently aversive that he stopped attending office hours altogether. He stuck it to me on my final evaluations, however. I can't be sure if it was his, but the evaluation with the lowest numerical ratings also contained the following telltale comment: "The instructor discouraged students from seeking help because, if they did, he then held them to a higher standard." The inanity of the comment speaks for itself. Still, the issue of how to provide formative feedback has plagued me ever since. Now I flat out refuse to read drafts, borrowing a justification from a senior colleague that "if I read a draft, it will turn *your* paper into *our* paper and I can't be a coauthor on a paper I'm also responsible for grading." In lieu of reading drafts, I let students know that I'm happy to answer any question at any time, but the only question I get is, "Why did you take off points?" on a paper that's already been graded. The response that some students seem to be expecting is "It was totally arbitrary" or "Because I hate you as a person," but that's only true some of the time.

LESSON 4: DON'T HAND BACK AN EXAM AT THE BEGINNING OF CLASS

Handing back an exam at the beginning of class is a rookie mistake, and I'm appalled I committed that mistake not once, not twice, but four times in my SFH. The exams not only distract students from attending to the material de jour, but students who did poorly on the exam will also glower at you for the remainder of class, if they don't outright revolt.

In my cog psych class, the handing back of exam 2 ended in a revolt. The leader was a student whom I'll call Cindy. Throughout the semester she had given not-so-subtle clues that she was unhappy with my instruction, like rolling her eyes at me when I moved through my lecture slides too quickly or attempting to point out inconsistencies between the lecture and the textbook. Early in the semester she came to office hours concerned about the grades she was getting on her papers (all in the B range); she wanted to know what exactly I was looking for. Midway through the meeting, she interjected an odd remark: "You know, Occidental is not the only college I got into. I also got into UCLA."

"That's nice," I said, looking at her quizzically.

"I got into UCLA," she continued, "because I'm a straight-A student. I don't get Bs. I've never gotten Bs. But for some reason, *in your class*, I'm getting Bs."

So there it was: Cindy was an intrinsically brilliant student, yet I had failed to glean that fact from her seemingly mediocre papers. I wanted to suggest that she wear a shirt emblazoned with "Straight-A Student"—or perhaps just a large scarlet A—so that no one else might make the same mistake. It wasn't true, I should add, that I was simply a harsh grader. A full third of the class had received As on the same assignments for which Cindy had received Bs. Cindy's papers were just not that good.

To help Cindy see the difference between her papers and the A papers, I printed one out and encouraged her to read it right then and there. She agreed that it was better than hers but maintained that hers was still A-level work. There was just no reasoning with Cindy. Unfortunately for Cindy (and me) she earned a C on exam 2. When I handed back the exams at the beginning of class, Cindy immediately tore into me, barking questions like "Why isn't C a correct answer to number 17?!" and "What exactly were you looking for in the third essay?!" Another student, whom I'll call Bobby, became emboldened by the outburst and joined in. Bobby had earned a D, making Cindy and him the poorest performers on the exam. But neither of them realized that. Rather, they assumed that everyone had done poorly and that the exam was thus flawed. Indeed, the flavor of their accusations quickly turned ugly. Cindy claimed my exams were too arbitrary ("You ask too many questions about unimportant details!"), and Bobby claimed they were too restrictive ("You don't give us the freedom to demonstrate our knowledge in our own way!"). This fifteen-minute outburst rendered the remaining forty minutes of class tense and awkward, not to mention the remaining four weeks of the semester. None of the other students joined in the smear campaign, but they were clearly affected by it. The class dynamic was irreparably altered.

To my surprise, Bobby sent an apologetic e-mail that evening, stating, "I didn't mean to come down on you at all today in class. My frustration has a lot more to do with my major on the whole than with the score I got on the test." Fair enough, but I would have preferred that my very *public* shaming were followed by a very *public* apology, perhaps in the form of a muffin basket presented in front of the entire class. Cindy, on the other hand, never apologized. She remained angry and sullen for the rest of the semester. Somehow, despite the fact that my exams were inherently flawed, she managed to earn an A+ on the final and, as a result, an A- in the course as a whole. Nevertheless, she refused to make eye contact with me the following semester when we encountered each other in passing.

Now I proactively avoid such wrath by handing back exams not only at the end of class but also with some statistical information about how the class did as a whole. Students who scored abnormally low thus *know* they've scored abnormally low, and they're much less inclined to make a fuss. It's hard to argue, after all, that an exam was inherently flawed when you're the only one who bombed it.

LESSON 5: DON'T MAKE BARGAINS OVER GRADES

Around the time of the Cindy-Bobby revolt, I handed back the second exam in my other class. It was not met with ire—at least not any overt ire—but it did bring one student to tears. That student, whom I'll call Jan, received the lowest grade in class (D-), which caused her to run out of the room sobbing, followed soon after by two girls who consoled her in the hall. I had expected displeasure from Jan, but I hadn't expected such *devastation*. In retrospect, I think Jan's theatrics were mainly for my benefit. Jan, it turns out, had a favor to ask at my next block of office hours. She wanted to be excused from answering all the math-based questions on the final exam. "I have a learning disability," she explained. "It wasn't an issue during the first exam because we hadn't covered anything involving numbers. But now that we're onto statistics, I'm having a lot of trouble."

"I see," I responded. "That would explain why you did so much better on the first exam than the second. What exactly is the nature of your learning disability?"

"I can't do math," she said.

"You can't do math?"

"No, I just can't do it. Anything with numbers confuses me. So I was wondering if, on account of my learning disability, I could just skip the statistics part of the final exam."

I explained to Jan that allowing her to skip a portion of the final exam would be unfair to the rest of the class, and I urged her to try her best at mastering the new material. That material was, after all, foundational to the follow-up course, Statistics, which was required for the major. Jan thanked me for my advice, but she left my office undeterred. Within a week, she had set up a meeting with the school's learning disabilities specialist and requested my presence.

The meeting was brief but memorable. The specialist confirmed that Jan did, indeed, have a learning disability and that I was obligated to make accommodations for her. When I asked the specialist what accommodations would be appropriate, she was unable—or unwilling—to make any specific recommendations. "That's up to you," she said. "You obviously know your course better than I do." I left that meeting quite perturbed, but Jan left seemingly uplifted. The specialist had not only legitimized her request but had placed the burden of how to accommodate Jan's learning disability squarely on my shoulders.

Sadly, I've now come to expect this burden as a regular part of teaching, most frequently incurred in the form of a cookie-cutter e-mail from the Office of the Dean of Students that reads,

> On [fill in the date], our office received documentation verifying that [fill in the name] had a temporary health condition in which a medical professional advised [him/her] to rest one to three days. Due to these instructions for care, this student might not have attended class during this time frame. To be clear, professors have the final decision on allowing students to complete missed assignments at a later time. However, given the nature of the student's absence, we encourage you to work with the student if possible.

Believe it or not, I get this e-mail about once a week. Being asked to adjust your teaching schedule and your grading requirements on a weekly basis can take its toll. My interpretation of the e-mail has thus become quite jaded, namely,

> Professor, we know you retain ultimate jurisdiction over your course, but don't be a dick. [Fill in the name] is special. Yes, it's true that other students in your course are likely suffering from similar afflictions, but those students did not have the gumption to seek out a formal request to shirk their responsibility. Please accommodate [fill in the name]'s request or you will be hearing from us again.

I didn't used to feel this way, but two experiences have changed my outlook. First, I've noticed that a disproportionate number of these notifications come on behalf of students whom I've independently verified as entitled and discourteous—that is, the Gregs and the Cindys of my classes. Second, when I consult with students on how to account for their tardy papers or missed exams, a good number offer the suggestion that the assignment be dropped altogether. That is, they don't want to make up the points; they want to pretend that the points were never lost in the first place.

And that's what Jan had requested. After our meeting with the learning disabilities specialist, she raised the possibility of skipping the math questions a second time, and when I balked once again, she raised a slightly different possibility: "What if I answer all the questions but if I do really bad on the math questions, you'll drop them from my grade?" At first, this new proposal struck me as equally repugnant, but on further reflection, I realized that it might serve to quell Jan's math anxiety without actually affecting her grade. Jan's poor performance on exam 2 was not, after all, due to the math questions. Jan had performed poorly on the entire exam, but her math anxiety led her to believe that the math questions were her one and only problem. I thus conceded to Jan's request, only to quickly regret it. Her performance on the math portion of the final was much worse than her performance on the math portion of exam 2. She answered almost every math question wrong. In fact, she was so consistently wrong that she would have done better if she had selected her answers at random. Apparently, Jan had decided to blow off the math-based material, since not knowing it wouldn't affect her grade. But she clearly studied the other material because her performance on the rest of the exam was stellar. Adding insult to injury, I later discovered an unsettling comment on my teaching evaluations, most certainly made by Jan: "The professor had little knowledge of how to deal with a student with a learning disability. He was unhelpful when I visited him in office hours to ask for assistance." To this day, the whole incident leaves a bad taste in my mouth, but I doubt that Jan has given it a second thought.

LESSON 6: DON'T LOSE SIGHT OF THE BIG PICTURE

Around the time of the Cindy-Bobby revolt and Jan's breakdown, my morale dropped precipitously. I began procrastinating from my teaching duties by searching for other jobs. I had had enough. Difficult students were one thing. But what drove me over the edge was dealing with those students *on top of* being exhausted from prepping six new lectures each week and grading two new assignments every other week. My schedule was packed. Mondays, Wednesdays, and Fridays were devoted to teaching and meetings; Tuesdays and Thursdays were devoted to prepping and grading. Research fell entirely by the wayside, which became yet another source of frustration.

The schedule might have been manageable if I weren't also swamped at home, raising a two-year-old child with a spouse whose job was as equally stressful as mine. All three of us were struggling with new transitions, and I just didn't have the stamina to deal with classroom management issues on top of my other responsibilities. What I failed to realize, however, was how inconsequential those issues really were. In time I would stop waking up on Monday thinking, *How the hell am I going to fill six hours of class time!*

The only lasting outcome of poorly managing my classroom that semester was a handful of negative teaching evaluations and two handfuls of bad memories, which, on the flip side, make good anecdotes at cocktail parties. Negative teaching evaluations are perhaps more problematic for me, on the tenure track at a liberal arts institution (where teaching is taken quite seriously), than for someone on the tenure track at an R1 institution. Still, every negative evaluation was accompanied by three to four positive evaluations, which begs the question of whether the negative ones should be trusted at all.

"It's good to reflect critically on your evaluations," a senior colleague once told me. "But don't let a bunch of eighteen-year-olds dictate what you do in your class. Kids that age don't have enough judgment to be allowed to buy alcohol or rent a car." My colleague's advice was comforting, but it didn't change the fact that these "irresponsible" eighteen-year-olds had the power to shape my tenure case.

It's hard not to begin viewing your students as your clients, or even as your boss. But to do so is, of course, a huge mistake. The only degree that faculty and students share in common is a high school diploma, and this gap in education and experience counts for much more than most students—and even some faculty—are willing to acknowledge. It's a gap that only truly becomes apparent to us all during commencement, when the graduating seniors don black, shapeless robes but the faculty don bright, colorful regalia, replete with ornate embroidery and a big poofy hat.

"Nice robes!" a graduating senior once shouted to me while waiting in line to receive his degree. "How do I get me some?"

"Five to ten years of graduate education," I shouted back. He snickered, oblivious to the demands of graduate school.

I was well aware of those demands coming into my SFH, yet one week in the classroom with a handful of discourteous students had somehow caused me to lose sight of all that I had achieved. I've now regained the confidence I lost during my SFH, but it hasn't been easy. Despite hopes that the worst bunch was behind me, the Gregs, Cindys, and Jans have persisted. They start with small requests, like granting an extension on a paper, and quickly move to larger requests, like postponing an exam, but I'm getting better at cultivating an air of authority that keeps such requests to a minimum.

Sometimes I think it would be simpler to just wear my regalia all year round, as a constant reminder of who's the boss. But doing so would be hot and uncomfortable in the Southern California sun. Maybe I'll just take to wearing the poofy hat instead.

8

PUBLISH, PERISH, OR APPLY FOR SOCIAL SECURITY

Reflections on the Tenure Process

Logan Greene

My plan, in case I was denied tenure, was to work as a Walmart greeter until I qualified for social security. I was much older than most tenure candidates, only a few years away from what normal people consider retirement age. The backup plan came to me during my frequent visits to Eugene, Oregon, to see my two adult daughters. While there, I was a regular at the Walmart across the street from Gold's Gym. My morning routine began with a workout, was followed by breakfast at Starbucks next door, and ended with a tour of the Walmart Superstore to pick up a pair of weightlifting gloves, a new skirt, or some other unnecessary delight. The greeter became my inspiration. She might have been seventy, with short, spiky hair and a sturdy build. When I walked in through the automatic doors, she flung her arms wide and called out with great cheer, "Welcome to Walmart!" She did this every morning. I felt very welcomed. I'm sure I shopped more aggressively because of her joyous greeting.

At home, trying to cope with the terror of my upcoming tenure deadline, I envisioned myself as a greeter, nodding at incoming shoppers while surreptitiously scanning their coats for illicit items and smiling at the ones who were once my students in Old English. I would be rigorously cheerful and yet as alert as many-eyed Argus, noting the departing shoppers with their bagged items and printed receipts. I would be friendly, yet alert; welcoming, yet commanding. I would work for a few years and then I would apply for social security with no deduction for earned income.

The imagined freedoms of working as a greeter sustained me as I worked toward tenure. I imagined a life in which I had weekends off, in which I did not contemplate an impossible workload every morning. I imagined taking lunch breaks, sitting around a table with my coworkers, instead of eating a protein bar in front of the computer. Would I miss the intellectual excitement of academic life? Would I find satisfaction in foiling shoplifters' attempts to conceal stolen goods under their coats? Would I develop an ambition to become a checkout clerk and be overwhelmed by the uncertainty of promotion? I calculated how much I actually earned as an assistant professor based on the hours I was working, and I realized that working at Walmart would almost certainly involve an increase in my hourly pay.

I pondered this plan as I waited for word of tenure. Of the three academic requirements of teaching, service, and scholarship, I was worried only about scholarship. I had over a decade of teaching experience by the time I entered my doctoral program, and my years of administrative work and community outreach made the service component of academia comfortable. My challenge would be getting published, and the path to achieving success as an author was opaque to me from the start. In my fifth year of graduate school, I gave a presentation at a national conference. A couple of weeks later I got a letter from one of the organizers expressing interest in my paper and asking me to submit it for publication. How exciting! I cried with relief, feeling validated and confident that I would succeed in this profession. I finished the paper and sent it off. I waited eagerly for a response. And waited. And waited. Fourteen months after I sent the paper, I received a rejection with no explanation.

I went on to submit four other papers, all based on coursework. None were accepted. Some came back with notes. Some of the notes were thoughtful and kind. Others were sarcastic and cruel. But I was not discouraged and felt sure that I would get the hang of it. Once I had a job, I worked like a maniac. Course preparation took many, many hours; in my first year, I probably spent fifty hours a week just on teaching. The remaining time was devoted to writing. I wrote on weekends, at night, and in the summer. I worked fourteen to sixteen hours per day, most days, at least eighty hours per week. Since I was granted a one-year extension of the standard six years to tenure, this schedule continued for seven years. As the years passed, rejections kept on coming, and the tenure deadline got closer and closer.

I completed, revised, and submitted essays to a variety of journals steadily from my first year. I had essays rejected for silly reasons, good reasons, and no reasons at all. Many rejections took years to arrive. Looking back on these years of intense and yet nearly fruitless struggles, I find that my failures had varied causes and involved anguish and drama, while my few successes were inexplicable nonevents. For the emerging (and veteran) academic, these publishing stories may sound eerily familiar.

THE SILENT TREATMENT

My first submitted paper was basically ignored and then ignored some more. It developed out of a conversation with graduate students in my first quarter as an assistant professor. With the students' permission, I presented this idea at a conference, after which the convener of my panel asked for full papers for a publication of conference proceedings. Thrilled at this opportunity, I completed the paper and sent it off to her. Months passed.

Hearing nothing from her, I wrote to ask for an update. "Still working on it," she replied. A few more months passed. I wrote again. I received no reply. Soon a year had passed. I wrote again. No reply. After a year and a half, I wrote again. She replied, "Still working on it." After three years, a professor colleague with more stature offered to contact her. A few days later, he informed me that my would-be editor had abandoned the project due to health problems. The whole ship had sunk, not just my contribution.

SLAP IN THE FACE

Not to be discouraged, I revised the essay for a different journal and sent it off. In my ignorance and growing desperation, I selected a journal that was wildly inappropriate for my essay. I should have seen the rejection coming: my work was theoretical and abstract while the journal was pedagogical and practical. This time, the article was rejected unambiguously with lightning speed: a two-week turnaround. A smack in the face! To his credit, the editor called me and explained why my work was not right for his purpose. This was one of the most helpful things that happened to me in the tenure process. His clarity underscored for me the need to pay attention to the scope of the journal to which I addressed my work. As one professor told me regarding tenure, "It's not so hard—you just publish a couple of things in regional journals, and you're in."

I came to understand that I had been like a young journalist starting out by sending work to the *New Yorker*. After that, I changed my focus and paid more attention to regional journals. I had already lost years because of editorial delay and carelessness; I could not afford to lose more time because of my own inattention. The vision of myself in a Walmart uniform haunted me. I would be such a good employee! I would always be on time for my shift! I would never make stupid mistakes like this!

CINDERELLA'S STEPSISTER

Then I found a call for papers that would be appropriate for my article with only minor revisions. This was an online journal, a new venue for me. By this time, I felt like Cinderella's stepsister forcing the tiny glass slipper onto her oversized foot: "I'll *make* it fit!" And it did. Four years after that conversation with my first graduate students, three and a half years after its first submission, my article was published. I had imagined that I would feel elated. But I only felt relief. By this time, two-thirds of the way into my probationary period, I was getting anxious about how long the publication process was taking. When I got the e-mail that started "Congratulations!" I immediately went to the website and downloaded my paper to put it in my tenure application file. Then, like the stepsister after Cinderella moved out, I tried to forget about it and move on. I would get better at finding glass slippers more my size.

JUMPING THROUGH HOOPS

My second foray into publishing as a tenure-track professor was also stimulated by an insightful remark from a student. Crediting her and the class, I composed an article and sent it off to a national journal. Then the games began. Submitting to this particular journal was an exercise in tedium and precision. The journal required a special font (jump). Special characters (archaic Middle English letters) needed to be indicated in a complicated manner (jump). Conforming to the style requirements took more hours than it had taken me to write the manuscript (jump). My article was rejected within four months—a fairly quick turnaround (or a pirouette?).

Despite the lack of any encouragement in the notes from the readers, I requested permission to resubmit. Sure, the editor said. I revised and revised and revised, slavishly adhering to every whim of the reviewers and jumping through hoop after hoop. Rejection . . . again. At that point, I had a year tied up in an unpublished essay, so I opted for "smaller" hoops and submitted the article to a regional publication and was rejected a year later. I revised the piece based on the comments and submitted it to a different regional journal. It was rejected in only five months.

Oddly, this was a kind of success. The whole process for this article from first submission to last rejection was three and a half years. All the while, as I revised and revised late into the night, I often browsed through the Walmart website to look at the job postings.

OPERATOR ERROR

Rejection on academic grounds is painful but understandable. Rejection due to my own error just hurts. For my third attempt, I selected a chapter of my dissertation and revised it to fit a national journal. Rejection in thirteen months. I revised and resubmitted to another national journal. When I had heard nothing after one year, I reviewed what I had submitted and discovered a silly mistake: I had given them my old graduate school e-mail address. Apparently I was losing my mind. Indeed, I moved on from this gaffe to write an essay on one of the *lais* of Marie de France even though I do not read French, modern or medieval. *Vous avez été rejeté* (You've been rejected). I assume that the editors rejected the article, though they didn't bother to contact me. Surely at Walmart there would be fewer opportunities to humiliate myself. Perhaps I could, on occasion, humiliate a careless shoplifter. Theft rejected!

KILLING ME SOFTLY, OR AT LEAST SLOWLY

The last submission I will recount was the wackiest of them all. I had finally realized that everything I had written, without exception, had a foundation in mythology. This led me to a lengthy search for journals that published in this area and an online publication by a university known for its creative programs in feminist thought and spirituality. I read the latest issue, which was suspiciously dated four years in the past. I called the institution for information. After half a dozen phone calls and a summer break of silence I learned that the journal was no longer being published. But wait! The director informed me that, in fact, it was! Foolishly encouraged by this information, I sent my essay to this journal. I heard nothing, followed by news about likely delays. Then a promising call for papers in a second journal came to my attention, so I wrote to the first journal and withdrew my paper from consideration. Of course, I heard nothing. But then after a couple of months I received a message: "Congratulations! Your paper has passed the second level of review and will be passed on to our editorial board for a final determination." Uh oh. Should I write back and tell them again that I had submitted the article to a different publication? Should I withdraw the article from the second publication? I decided to let things ride to see what would happen. What happened was nothing. My paper was rejected by the second journal, and the first journal never contacted me again.

TO BOOK OR NOT TO BOOK...

The most humiliating and frustrating part of my tenure process was the publication of a book. Surely this should have been my greatest joy. Instead, this experience caused me such pain that I almost didn't write about it. At a regional conference, I came across a publisher's representative who was asking about manuscripts ready for publication. I hesitated. Was this really a respected academic publisher? Should I wait and try for a more competitive publisher? A colleague urged me to submit my dissertation to them. Back home, I looked at the publisher's website and realized that I had two books in my library that they had published. The books were beautifully produced and were both scholarly works. Hearing time's winged chariot at my back, I sent them a proposal, which they accepted. I revised my dissertation over a period of three months and sent it in.

My department's personnel committee scrutinized this publication closely. Could it be considered peer reviewed? Should it count at all? Eventually, they established that the publisher had used a peer-review process, and they counted the book toward tenure. The dean was less amenable; she eventually passed me but with sharp criticisms of the lack of competitiveness of the publisher. I was torn between the humiliation of this widespread and public criticism and the anguish of recognizing that without this inadequate publication I would not have achieved the requirements for tenure. Is this what success feels like?

My tenure application was a miscellaneous assortment of published essays, course observations, student evaluations, letters of recommendation, a hardback book, and a collection of cards, charts, and plaques. I turned in this gigantic pile of academic stuff and immediately fell apart. The six months after I turned in the tenure application were lost to anxiety as I waited to know my fate. When I finally received the congratulatory e-mail from the provost in May, I was stunned with relief. Over break I went to Eugene to visit my daughters. I idled, went to the gym, and visited Walmart. I studied the enthusiastic greeter, who was still at work.

Tenure was followed by election to my current position as department chair. It's not unusual that ten or eleven hours spent staring at piles of incomprehensible paperwork are punctuated by an endless stream of students complaining about grades, faculty members, and graduation requirements and faculty members complaining about schedules, course assignments, and students.

Two days ago I had meetings from eight-thirty in the morning until five o'clock in the afternoon. I ate lunch through a meeting with a thesis student, dripping Thousand Island dressing on her papers. And then it occurred to me, *This was my reward for seven years of eighty-hour work weeks filled with constant anxiety about losing my job: more eighty-hour work weeks and the promise that they would never end.* Thankfully, I only have one more year until I apply for social security. And I have to admit, being a Walmart greeter never looked better.

9

THE LIFE OF THE MIND ... IN THE COMPANY OF OTHERS

Amanda Jansen

It's probably best to start off like this: *Hi, my name is Mandy, and I am an extrovert.* I am overly enthusiastic about making friends through work. Interacting with people is a source of energy for me. When I hear my friends describe the ways that being a professor doesn't match up to their ideal image of what they thought this job would be, I don't relate.

Many of my friends describe their vision of being a professor like this: They would enjoy extended time reading in coffee shops and libraries. They would relish every chance to puzzle through intellectual dilemmas and develop ideas, sometimes while riding their bikes, running, or walking. They would take advantage of every opportunity for extended time to write and think. They say that their lived experience played out differently from this vision. They have expressed frustration about the extensive amount of service tasks that encroach upon their efforts to write and be academically creative.

Although I also cherish my research time, I am looking for something slightly different than what they describe. I am looking for a community. I love it when people gather around a table and excitedly share different takes on a data set or brainstorm new ways to outline an idea for a paper. For me, one of the joys of being a researcher has been the opportunity to collaborate. Research has been, in part, a way for me to connect with others over ideas. I, too, crave more time for research in my daily professional work, but I also long for interpersonal connection. Yes, I want to live the life of the mind . . . but in the company of others.

People know this about me. It's not a secret. A few years back, I returned to the university where I attended graduate school to give a colloquium to faculty and doctoral students. My former advisor introduced me with heartfelt sincerity. He said, "I would like to introduce my friend and colleague, Amanda Jansen. If you ask Mandy about her job, one of the first things she'll tell you is how much she enjoys working with her colleagues." Then he went on to describe my interesting coworkers before introducing me and my work. This was an appropriate approach, I thought. It helped the audience at the colloquium learn more about my university, not just about me. It's true; I am fond of my colleagues. And I got a bit emotional when my former advisor publicly called me his friend.

But my longing for community can create problems for me in the workplace. My enthusiasm for fostering interpersonal relationships with colleagues can bubble over the top. My priorities get misdirected. By this I mean that rather than developing relationships while working on research, service, or teaching, sometimes building relationships becomes the end goal in itself. Building relationships becomes my work rather than an incidental secondary outcome.

POSTER OR SOCIAL HOUR

There have been times when I have posed as if I was engaged in research, but my ulterior motive was to connect with others. As a result, I missed some chances to push my thinking about my research because I was focused on fostering friendships. One of those instances was when I presented a poster at a conference. Preparing for conferences is a perfect storm that builds up my need for the company of others. I underestimate all that needs to be done before a conference. During my conference preparation time, I lose balance. I become overworked and deprived of interpersonal interaction. By the time I arrive at the conference, I am so happy to just see people that I end up pouncing on them.

Consider a recent poster session: The session is about to begin. The researchers have carefully tacked or clipped their posters to their stands. They make last-minute adjustments to straighten them. Many of them mentally rehearse a one- or two-minute long verbal abstract about their study to share; anticipate questions they might be asked about their work; and think about questions and wonderments to pose to people who might visit their posters. The audience members at the poster session scan the room and consider which poster to visit as they consult the map and layout of the room as well as the titles of posters in their conference programs.

While most presenters and attendees are focused on what they would learn about research from participating in the poster session, on this occasion I bopped up and down on my tiptoes and became more gleeful by the moment. After weeks and weeks of sequester and solitude, sweet release! I was about to be surrounded by lots of interesting people. Who would come visit me at my poster? Who would I get to see? Who would I meet? Which old friends would I encounter? I was about to thrive with an hour and a half of social time! I anticipated some prime time in a salon of ideas and personal connections.

My first visitor approached and started to read my poster. I wondered, *Should I interrupt?* I shifted my weight from one foot to another, waiting for her to speak first. After a few moments, she did:

Visitor: So, I was reading, and I was curious about . . .

Me: Hi! I'm Mandy! Thanks for coming to my poster. It's nice to meet you! What are you working on lately? How are you?!

Visitor: Um . . .

The visitor hesitated a bit, and then she shared some thoughts about her own professional work. Perhaps she did not hear the lingering warning in the air: *step away from the hyper girl, for she also has an ulterior motive.* It's like a bait and switch. Show up for the exchange of ideas and leave with a new acquaintance, potentially a new friend. This was an awkward moment, because the poster attendee was there to talk about my research study, and my expectations were more along the lines of social bonding.

I should know better than to treat a poster at a conference like a receiving line. Sometimes I think that I should avoid poster presentations altogether. For me, the temptation to meet, greet, and socialize is too great. People are there to discuss the scholarly ideas, not to chitchat, right? Well, you might think that, but I spent the majority of the time at my most recent poster session talking with other people about their lives outside of work and *their* research rather than talking about my own poster. More formal presentations would probably be better for focusing on research ideas, as it's harder to bond with new and old friends when you're sitting in uncomfortable hotel chairs and staring at text-laden slides.

Afterward, I was disappointed with myself. I usually enjoy conferences at least in part because of the opportunity to push my own work forward through discussion. Yet spending my poster session talking with everyone else about their work did not help my own progress as much as, you know, *talking about my actual poster* would have done. I missed the opportunity to learn from others, but I fostered my relationships. This is a tension I face: how can I meet my high needs for interpersonal connection in my work as an academic while respecting that others do not have the same high need for social bonding at work?

THE SOCIAL COMMITTEE

I have looked to my service work and committee meetings as another way to fulfill my need to strengthen and build relationships. Often I see my weekly schedule and it has far too many committee meetings on it, but my response to my full schedule is not disdain. Rather, I look forward to meetings. They are a chance to get out and see people. Meetings leave me feeling less isolated. I have had the experience of looking at my calendar and thinking, "Yay! At this meeting, I will see my friend, and maybe we can talk before or after the meeting or something! And at this other meeting, I don't really know anyone, because it's my first meeting on this university-level committee, and I'm kind of nervous, because I totally want to make a good impression on these people. Okay, so they probably won't even remember my name after the meeting, but still . . . what if I become really good friends with one of the committee members?! Won't that be FUN?!"

It's probably more typical for faculty to arrive at a committee meeting with an air of wanting it to end as soon as possible. It's common to arrive late, because we're all overscheduled. Even if people arrive on time, they multitask during the meeting. They grade or review a journal article or read a draft of a graduate student's dissertation chapter. Some people daydream and stare out the window, imagining all of the other things that they would rather be doing. The whooshing sound of sent e-mails punctuates the committee conversations. I suppose that most academics look at meetings as necessary but not pleasant. Little do they know that their moments of disengagement are potentially interfering with my personal agenda: make new friends and keep the old.

One day it dawned on me that I view attending committee meetings differently from other faculty—as a speed-dating approach to finding a new friend. I am usually one of the first to arrive. I am alert and overprepared, hoping to impress someone enough to get an invitation to go to coffee or lunch later that day or week. I get settled and comfortable, review the agenda, and look forward to seeing who will arrive next. As a colleague walks into the room, I engage him or her in conversation. I try to remember something about her or his family or preferred hobby to help my colleague see that I value her or his friendship. During this dialogue, another colleague will have entered the room, so I turn to greet him or her with a compliment, perhaps mentioning how the choice of that color of sweater is a nice contrast to his or her eyes. Then I try to engage the group around us in a bit of an exchange about how our weeks are going. At this point, I start to give updates about my life and hope that some of us feel some sort of connection. Basically, I co-opt the start of the meeting to build my social network.

It turns out that a perfect committee for finding a potential new friend is a faculty search committee. What?! You don't look at a faculty search as an audition for Mandy's Next New Best Friend Forever? What could be better—regular meetings, a big pool of potential friends, er, applicants, and work-funded drinks and meals!

We hired a new faculty member in my program area the year after I was hired, and she and I became great friends, the kind that when I got into a car accident, she picked me up at the scene and insisted that I sleep over at her house with her family rather than stay alone that night. We have gone in and out of each other's offices as needed to debrief from meetings, talk about teaching and research, and create research collaborations so that we can spend more time together.

Our first opportunity to build our friendship didn't happen during her interview as I had hoped it would. During that particular hiring season, I was frustrated, because I was out of town during Tonya's interview. I did not get to meet a candidate and make a good impression! I had hoped that if our prospective colleagues would be able to meet me during their interviews, they would realize that a benefit of working in my department, in my program area, would be having me as a colleague. Because I am happy! And friendly! And upbeat! And encouraging! And so supportive! I was going to be the friend that she did not yet know that she wanted.

I watched Tonya's research colloquium on video to learn a bit about her work. Although I appreciated the ideas in her talk and was intrigued by them, I also thought, *Hey, we could be friends.* That's right, it's all about *my social needs*. But after grad school, there are not many other opportunities to enter into a community with other people at the same time and go through intense bonding transition experiences with people who are relatively close to your age and stage in life. I thought that it would be a great way to bond with someone, by going through professional experiences together and supporting each other. She would be entering academia right around the same time that I did, and we would be right around the same age. Perfect! She wanted a job. I wanted another friend. This was a win-win situation, right?

Although I did not get to meet Tonya during her job interview, I developed a plan: we would meet at an upcoming conference. I saw that she had a presentation on the program, and I had one, too. And even better, her presentation was a poster, so . . . social hour! Little did she know, but she had arranged for a work version of speed-dating-for-friends when she decided to present a poster, and I happily planned to sidle up to her as a potential date.

When the day arrived, I had been looking forward to meeting Tonya in person so much that I was, of course, early to arrive at her poster session. I spotted her from a distance. I quickly walked (almost ran) up and gave her a big hug. But I had forgotten that we had not met in person yet. Since I had spent so much time thinking about meeting her, by that point we were already friends in my mind. I began our new impending friendship by stalking and then assaulting her.

Graciously, Tonya laughed and didn't hold my forwardness against me. I released her from my hug and then bumbled around to announce that I was her new colleague and that I was *so pleased to meet her! And how was she doing?!* I also asked her about her study, but I remember more about love bombing her than I do about the content of her poster.

Even though I am mortified by the memory of how eager I was to meet her, Tonya insists that she remembers me as welcoming. I do try to model openness and a welcoming, inclusive spirit, so I was glad that she attributed positive intentions toward me. I figure that her options were to either appreciate my good intentions or to press charges. Luckily for me, she chose the former.

LEFT OUT

While teaching recently, I looked out into the hallway through the open door, and I saw some senior professors, a center director, my dean, and other colleagues headed down the hallway into a conference room. Immediately, I wondered, "What is happening? And why was I not invited? Is everyone having fun without me? How can I be a part of whatever that is?" Keep in mind, I noticed this *while I was teaching*. It's not like I was sitting in my office with my door open, my mind wandering, and hoping to be distracted. This took place during one of my classes. There were undergrads that I had a responsibility to teach right in front of me. Yet I still noticed this group of people walking past me, and I felt left out.

Why was that my first reaction? Some people would not have noticed that there were people walking past the open door, let alone noticed who was walking by. Most people probably would not have worried about it. Other people may have noticed their colleagues gathering down at the end of the hallway and would have been happy to have been exempt from another meeting. Me? I wanted to be included.

I even sought out information about the meeting after my class was over. I asked colleagues about what had been scheduled in that particular conference room at that particular time. I realized that it was a talk related to a search for a director of another campus center, and I had overlooked the e-mail invitation to attend because it conflicted with my teaching. I was never excluded in the first place!

COPING WITH MY NEED FOR SOCIAL TIME

I considered not pursuing a job in academia after graduate school because I crave so much social interaction in my daily life. In many ways, this line of work requires solitary spaces. Much of our work is done in private, even when there are collaborative aspects to it: data analysis and writing, lesson planning and grading—the solitary tasks go on and on. Although I enjoy these intellectual endeavors, I also go stir crazy if I do not balance them out with a lot of social time.

I am constantly seeking the social side of academia. I put a lot of energy into weaving social spaces through workspaces. For good or bad, most of my friends are from work. Although I don't always make balanced choices, I do my best to err on the endearing side of eager.

Most people are probably looking to, you know, *work* at work. They may consider their dance cards to be already full with a partner, family, and friends from outside of work. In contrast, I probably try to overbook my dance card. I attempt to blend my personal and professional sides of my life a bit too much at times. I want my colleagues to want to be my friends, even when cultivating our friendship isn't on their radar screens. For them, accomplishing work tasks is likely to be the priority. Sure, that's important to me, too, but also—let's be friends. Such good friends! I'll see you at our next meeting. Maybe we can have lunch afterward. What do you think?

III

Professors Are People, Too

The interrelationship of life and work is in part a persistent mystery. There is an episode of the idyllic 1950s television show *Leave It to Beaver* titled "Teacher Comes to Dinner" in which Ward and June Cleaver invite Miss Landers to their house for a family meal. Upon learning of the impending event, Beaver's friend Larry is so intrigued that he decides to charge his friends Whitey and Gilbert a quarter to hide in a tree and spy on Miss Landers. When Miss Landers arrives at the house, Beaver tells her eagerly, "This is where I live when I'm not at school!" When the family sits down to dinner, the three boys provide a secret running commentary from a nearby tree:

"Look now, she's eating an onion!"

"How about that!"

"What are those things hanging from her ears?"

"This isn't worth a quarter."

"Who wants to see her eating dessert?"

"After dessert she might even smoke!"

"That would be worth a quarter to see that!"

"Look, she's got toes! There, coming right out of her shoes!"

Eventually, while Ward and June are clearing up the dishes, Miss Landers confronts the boys and asks what they are doing in the tree.

"Gee Miss Landers," says Larry, "none of us saw a teacher eat before." Miss Landers, in her infinite 1950s wisdom, smiles and tells the boys, "Sometimes it's hard for boys to realize that a teacher thinks and acts like a real person." Beaver replies, "Boy, you sure are acting like a real person tonight!" [Cue audience laughter.]

Beaver's comment is sweetly naive, though it can sometimes seem as though the general public similarly forgets that educators, both teachers and professors, are people, too. Images of professors as full-time occupants of the Ivory Tower do not lend themselves well to envisioning what professors' lives are like outside the university. Where do they live when they are not at school? What do they eat? How do they manage their families with their academic lives? How do their stodgy academic ways of viewing the world function when they bump into everyday life? And do they have toes?

In this section, five authors provide insight into these answers—what happens when professors, or burgeoning academics, are out in society and, in the words of Miss Landers, thinking and acting like real people. Some of the authors explore what happens when the theoretical perspectives that seem to carry so much power at the university encounter reality, while others reflect upon the rough fit between an academic's life and the incessant—and at times inconvenient—needs of our own offspring.

10

THE VILLAGE IDIOT

Erin Marie Furtak

My favorite story from my husband Dave's study abroad in Germany is about his visit to the doctor's office for an MRI on his shoulder. His German wasn't great at the time, and when the nurse uttered a flurry of instructions in a thick Bavarian dialect, all he could understand were the words "pants" and "out." Confused but compliant, Dave removed his clothing and waited, naked from the waist down, for the nurse to return. When she came back, she gaped at him in horror and screamed, in the clearest *Hochdeutsch* my husband has ever heard, "I said to take the *change* out of your *pants pockets*!"

In retrospect, I should have regarded this anecdote as more of an omen when I sent off my application to the Humboldt Foundation for funding to support postdoctoral educational research in Germany. My husband and I boarded a plane a week after I received my PhD, Dave an out-of-practice Germophone, and I a dangerous novice with little more than a couple of Goethe Institute courses and the comforting knowledge that I had become a "certified" member of the academic cognoscenti.

As I stepped off the plane, I simultaneously moved from the top of one educational ladder to the lowest rung of another. I had traded in my velvet robe, hood, and poofy hat for a threadbare, dingy-white T-shirt that said "Village Idiot."

Dave and I moved first to Bonn, where the Humboldt Foundation had graciously enrolled all of the new fellows and their spouses in language classes for eight hours a day, five days a week, for two months prior to settling in Berlin. Dave's years of German study paid off and landed him in the top-level conversation course with other former German majors, whereas my evening and weekend courses had landed me in only the second-lowest class. It was comforting that there was at least one group that I could look down upon.

It was the summer of the World Cup, and a sweltering heat wave had settled into the Rhine Valley. The language courses were held in a house that had formerly served as an embassy building in the government quarter during Bonn's postwar glory days as capitol, and the language school's proprietor proudly told us that we would be learning our new language behind tank-proof windows. This was of course no comfort given the lack of air conditioning in the building (a sticker in the restroom boasted that Germany was the "World Champion of Energy Conservation").

Thus it was in a small room behind four-inch-thick glass and in a fog of BO that I spent my summer. In the sweltering heat we were introduced to our instructor, Mark, a chain-smoking rugby player who existed on nothing but apples, yogurt, and beer. Mark embraced the moment and told us with a glimmer in his eye that this was a perfect opportunity to learn the German word for hot and humid weather: *schwül*. Mark had us practice making the umlaut sound by puckering up our lips and really getting into that *ü* sound. *Schwül, schwül, schwül*, we chanted together.

As I hung out after class on the front steps of the school, I resolved to try out my new word on someone. As the students from Dave's class filtered out the front door, I sidled up to his classmate, Ed, smiling broadly and informing him, *"Es ist schwul."* He guffawed heartily before he told me to be careful. Apparently, if you mess up the *ü* sound and pronounce it like an American, you get an entirely different word altogether that is slang for homosexual.

Furthering my humiliation, Ed was actually *schwul*, but fortunately also good-natured and didn't seem to mind. This was the first of many experiences that showed me over and over again that what I thought I knew about learning—the very field in which I was supposedly expert—was a little more complicated than I had thought.

MOTIVATION + CONTEXT = LEARNING

A major focus of educational reform has been in making learning environments more authentic, or tied to the real world outside the school walls.[1] Research has also indicated that tapping into students' motivation and interest in a subject can help them to learn.[2] My graduate school officemate Colin used to joke that he needed a "No Shit" stamp for papers that came to what we thought were commonsense conclusions like these. People who want to learn will learn more. If learning in school is more like life, then people will use it in their lives—*no shit*.

Now as a learner myself—a stranger in a strange land—I found that such commonsense research findings were easier to study than to live and led to many moments where I could have used a different stamp to mark my experiences that said, *oh shit*. It would have ultimately been more appropriate for my experience because, unfortunately, what seemed like commonsense research findings did not translate easily to my lived experience.

I wanted to learn German, I really did. And I was living in Germany, surrounded by native speakers and the written word everywhere, and I was supposed to just drink up the language like so many *Weißbeere* on long, summer evenings in the *Biergarten*. But German is really, really hard, and really, really complicated, almost as though the language were constructed with a set of arcane foundational rules underlying layer upon layer of exceptions, just to make sure that *Ausländer* have no chance whatsoever to penetrate the local culture. Despite the German fondness for rules, they seem to delight in those exceptions, even calling verbs that resist the rules *stark*, or strong.

My classmates Wyly and Andrew took to high-fiving each other if they got more than five out of ten right on the daily *der/die/das* quiz. The bar was suddenly embarrassingly low, and it didn't matter where I was, or how much I wanted to learn (or, in many cases, how hard I tried). Success did not come easily. One evening after a particularly hard day in class, when hauling a cartful of empty glass bottles back to the supermarket, I hit a big crack in the sidewalk and sent the bottles tumbling and breaking all over the street. I crouched on the curb and started to cry. Ed happened to be nearby and rushed over and comforted me. He assured me that I would get this whole *schwul/schwül* thing figured out eventually.

METACOGNITION OF LEARNING PROCESSES

Many educational psychologists have spoken about the importance of being cognitive of one's own thinking and learning processes.[3] The idea is that if you pay attention to what you know and what you have left to learn, it will help you to chart your progress and take ownership of your own learning. Well, it was pretty clear when I got to Bonn that I had no idea what the hell I was saying or doing.

Starting at such a low place, it was easy to chart my slow, incremental progress. When I started, I just wanted to throw out words that I knew, usually in the middle of conversations to show that I agreed (*Ja, stimmt*) or things around me that I could identify, usually those with easy cognates in English (*apfel*! [apple]). In "Me Talk Pretty One Day," David Sedaris called this the "evil baby" stage of language acquisition.[4] (See *schwül* above.)

So you can imagine that I felt like a big shot when Mark taught me the keys to making a sentence in German: the verb is always in the second position—oh, unless it is in a dependent clause. Or unless there is more than one verb, in which case there would be both a verb in the second position and a verb at the end. Wait, what? To a person accustomed to speaking English, this basically means starting your sentence with a subject and your first verb, and then throwing in all the other direct objects, indirect objects, adjectives, articles, and other stuff before putting your final, conjugated verb at the end.

I was soon speaking in labored, grammatically incorrect sentences and more often than not would wind my way to the end of the sentence and forget what verb I had meant to use. Impatient Germans would cut me off and speak to me in perfect English, hoping to head me off at the chase, while their more gracious countrymen would lean forward expectantly and then, as I nervously stuttered and reversed the sentence in my head to remember where I had started, say the verb to save me from myself.

At about this time Angela, Dave's host mother from his study abroad, told me that to a German ear, I sounded like Yoda. Progress, this was?

Toward the end of the summer, I had a larger vocabulary, but my communication process was still excruciatingly slow: hear German, translate in head to English, think about what to say in English, devise response in English, translate to German, think of word order, and respond in German. It was honestly easier to fake it rather than eke it out stepwise as I had been doing before. There were things I heard all the time that were in the right order that I would just start saying so people would think I was learning something. This didn't mean I had much understanding of the gender of words (God, don't even get me started) or the word order, just that I was good at memorizing things. It was sort of like audio flashcards, which—as a good scholar of high-quality learning environments—I of course looked upon with abhorrence. But I could show off by making jokes about things I heard around Berlin and impress my friends with how good my German was getting, when really I just had a good memory for things I heard over and over on the U-Bahn. Things like "My name is Dirk Armmann. I have for three months out of work been. I plead you a small donation." Or "Please beware you when getting off the gap between the train and platform."

It wasn't until the leaves, grown fat and large from the steamy summer, were turning a dingy brown under the flat Berlin sky that the characters in my dreams started speaking German. Somehow I had this amazing clarity in my subconscious that evaded me in my waking hours—people would speak German to me, and I not only understood them but also would artfully and fluently respond.

Around this same time I found myself skipping steps in communication—hear German, respond in German, or as I call it, hearing and understanding. But at this point I was still only speaking when spoken to, walking around Berlin in a bubble of English with my American husband, American friends, American TV shows, and American podcasts, only breaking into German when it was absolutely necessary. My dream self apparently didn't know she was American.

At the end of our second summer in Berlin, I felt that I was making progress. Many neighborhood streets are made of jawbreaking, bone-rattling cobblestones that are awful to ride over on a bike, while the sidewalks are smooth, concrete pavers. Usually bicyclists are restricted to riding in designated lanes or in the street, but there was one particular stretch of street where I just couldn't take it and routinely popped my bike onto the sidewalk to avoid the jolting. On this day I narrowly missed a man getting out of his car, and as he jumped back he shouted at me, "*Warum können Sie nicht auf die Straße wie andere Menschen fahren!?"* (Why can't you ride on the street like other people!?). Aside from my amusement at how Germans labor even to shout at people on the street (a comparable New Yorker would have just yelled an obscenity), I was also delighted that I had understood his every word. Of course, a more fluent speaker would have had a snappy retort (such as the *"Kann schön, will nicht"* [I could but don't want to] Angela later suggested).

It took a while, but over time I had small signs of improvement. Germans love technology—self-cleaning toilet seats, intelligent recycling machines, and automated soft-serve ice cream machines—which makes for many unsolicited interactions, mainly about why the machines are broken. This was especially true in Berlin. I had just learned that the bottle recycling machine was down at our local grocery store when a heavily tattooed and pierced, Dirk-like man tried to put a bottle in the machine one day. I found myself leaning over and telling him, *"Es ist kaput gegangen."* I had come a long way.

LEGITIMATE PERIPHERAL PARTICIPATION

One of the major theories of learning in educational research is referred to as situative, meaning that all learning is situated in particular environments and is facilitated by social interactions.[5] A component of this theory is referred to as the "apprenticeship of observation" and is illustrated by thinking about the process of learning to be a tailor. First an apprentice learns how to cut patterns, but more experienced tailors do the garment construction and sewing. Over time, the apprentice learns, step by step, to take measurements, sew hems, and finally to fit garments and sew more complicated seams.

When I apprenticed to the experienced German speakers, it reinforced my feeling like the village idiot, because everywhere—on TV, on the streets, and even in school—all I saw were people who were doing much better than me. On one episode of *Germany's Next Topmodel*—such was the high-quality TV I was able to comprehend—there was an American judge, and I couldn't wait for him to open his mouth and hear what was sure to be a terrible accent. And yet, when he did speak, the German vowels flowed out beautifully, and I began to hate him. Can't I even watch reality TV for some escape?

Even the seven- and nine-year-old daughters of some of the Russian Humboldt fellows were picking up the language faster than me. Since they didn't speak English, and I couldn't remember any of the four years of Russian I had supposedly studied in high school, we communicated with them in German. One day I glared jealously at Anya as she told me that her money was in *die Tasche*. What! How did she know *Tasche* was feminine?

Supposedly, one can see others at the same level of competence, full proficiency (e.g., with native German speakers), and all stages in between, and thereby see not only the goal but also how far one has come. For example, I always found it easiest to talk in German with those at my same level, who made the same mistakes as I did, but forcing myself to speak to Germans helped train my ear to different accents, to learn new words, and to correct my mistakes.

When my family and friends came to visit and I was called upon to lead interactions with dry cleaners, make reservations, and translate tour guides, I realized I had come a long way, until my friend Alicia—having been here for three weeks—said she could tell she was learning German because the bus driver corrected her, as he always did me. Thanks a lot.

RISK TAKING

As a teacher, I was always instructed to create a classroom climate in which students felt safe to take risks, and to treat mistakes kindly, so that making mistakes could be learning experiences. I knew this was important, but as someone who did well in school, the sense of risk didn't take on full meaning until I learned German—a task that did not come to me as easily as other subjects I have studied. I wanted to understand everything, but that was not possible, so when someone spoke to me, I needed to learn how to take risks, not only by asking questions, but also by taking action on what I thought I had understood.

In my first days at the Research Institute in Berlin where I was to work, a kind member of the Director's Secretariat gave me a tour of the important elements of my working life in the clearest Berlin dialect she could muster. A thick haze of cigarette smoke hung in the building's circuitous hallways as we wandered to and fro, and I was relieved to discover that the bounds of her instructions adhered closely to the chapters in my German textbook: here is the ladies' restroom, here is the place where you can get coffee, office supplies are kept in this cabinet, and so forth.

At the end of the tour she took an abrupt right turn into what would be my office and went off-script. She leaned over my desk and pointed to the standard-issue telephone, stared deeply into my eyes, and said slowly, "It is very, very important that you do not forget to [X]." I nodded and smiled with enough confidence that she patted me on the arm and breezed out, but as I replayed the sentence in my mind, I was horrified to discover that I had no idea what [X] meant. I stood and stared at the phone, which no longer sat idly atop my desk, but whose blinking red and green buttons now taunted me with some mysterious, incredibly urgent purpose. What could be so important to do with the phone that it would rate on the same level as knowing where the ladies' room was located? I thought back over the sentence in my head. Maybe she said that it was very, very important that I *not* do something, not that I *not forget* to do something. What should I not do? Should I never make long, homesick phone calls to my parents in the United States? Should I never answer it since my German was so terrible, lest I embarrass the Herr Doktor Professor Direktor of the Institute?

As I relive this event, I find myself leaning as if at a horror movie with a noncompliant heroine, screaming, "You village idiot! Just walk three doors down the hallway and march into the Secretariat and ask all those *Frauen* in there what [X] means!" But of course, this was too scary. I was trying to pass myself off as knowledgeable, and surely [X] was a pretty important word that I should have learned in my two months' hard labor at the ex-embassy in Bonn. Ironically, and in a nod to the inanity of institutional and office life, I never figured out what [X] was and it never seemed to matter.

Despite the progress I made, my triumphs were always mingled with mistakes and reminders of my status as a novice. I missed a conference call late in the summer after taking the wrong bus from the train station, wandering around for forty-five minutes in the hot, sweaty heat—yes, it was *schwul*, wait, no, *schwül*—after misinterpreting the directions I had so bravely ventured to ask in my best German.

Another morning I didn't pronounce the word for *Mohnschnecke*, one of my favorite breakfast pastries, to the baker's liking, and she loudly corrected me while the regular patrons turned to check out the weirdo who didn't know her *Mohnschnecken* from her *Schweineörchen*.

In the end, the most important lesson I learned may not have been any particular German *Unterricht* but lessons about learning itself. That is, the researcher's *no shit* conclusions can't capture the learner's *oh shit* experiences. What I thought I knew, what I was supposed to be expert in, took on new meaning when I was repositioned as a newbie myself. Learning anything new—anything worth knowing—inevitably involves moments of effort, confusion, and failure. Sometimes you learn, and sometimes you lose your pants; but if you have faith in the learning process, you'll always be able to put your pants back on and face the world anew.

NOTES

1. See Jrene Rahm, Heather C. Miller, Laurel Hartley, and John C. Moore, "The Value of an Emergent Notion of Authenticity: Examples from Two Student/Teacher-Scientist Partnership Programs," *Journal of Research in Science Teaching* 4, no. 8 (2003): 737–56.

2. COACTIV-Projekt am Max Planck Institut für Bildungsforschung, Berlin, "Professionswissen von Lehrkräften, kognitiv aktivierender Mathematikunterricht und die Entwicklung mathematischer Kompetenz," May 2011, https://www.mpib-berlin.mpg.de/coactiv/index.html.

3. See Barbara Y. White and John R. Frederiksen, "Inquiry, Modeling, and Metacognition: Making Science Accessible to All Students," *Cognition and Instruction* 16, no. 1 (1998): 3–118.

4. David Sedaris, "Me Talk Pretty One Day," in *Me Talk Pretty One Day*, 166–73 (Cambridge, MA: Back Bay Press, 2001).

5. See Jean Lave and Etienne Wenger, *Situated Learning: Legitimate Peripheral Participation* (Cambridge: University of Cambridge Press, 1991); and L. S. Vygotsky, *Mind in Society: The Development of Higher Psychological Processes* (Cambridge, MA: Harvard University Press, 1978).

11

HOT MESS TIMES THREE

Hindi Krinsky

When I found out I was expecting triplets, my life as a productive graduate student effectively ended. For the next twenty-four months, I embarked on a hamster's wheel of sonograms, vomit, and advisor meetings. For anyone searching for the ultimate method of procrastination, triplets are a slam dunk. Not even an exciting dissertation topic, like researching the textual affordances of graphic novels, can compete with discovering that your three toddlers have used your research protocols as a gigantic coloring book.

When I first realized I was pregnant, my mother begged me to be responsible and go for a sonogram. I pushed it off for weeks. My husband David and I were both in graduate school, our first child in many ways, and we didn't have time to navigate NYC traffic and procure the appropriate insurance referrals. I continued to push off the appointment until my mother publicly announced at a family event, "Don't be offended, but you're beginning to look like a runaway train with an extra caboose."

Soon thereafter, my mother was having prophetic dreams of me giving birth to twins. My grandmother phoned daily to inquire after "the babies." My sister began discussing pairing names: Brangelina? The time had come to put an end to these superstitious and scuttle(big)butt rumors. After a final public humiliation involving a gift of stretched clothing, I decided that I'd had enough.

With my feet in stirrups, waiting for the triumphant drumroll that would prove my mother wrong, the sonographer gasped, screeched, and then dropped the little magic wand right out of my vagina. My face shot to the grainy screen, *three bubbles . . . three windows? What the heck was I looking at?* Although I was well informed about my arcane area of research, I hadn't the faintest clue what the inside of my own body looked like.

Although my mother's otherworldly visions told me to expect multiples, I still found myself sucked into a vortex of shock. I cried and laughed to the steady beating of their three barely existent hearts. Of course, the most surprising part was that my mother had been right. In addition to forcing me to rethink my formal position on dreams, this bombshell shattered my neat (ok, messy) little world of papers, deadlines, and beer. In reality, no degree can ever prepare you for life's random fly balls or, in my case, an unexpected litter of children.

Fortunately, the triplets weren't my first foray into the world of the strange. I had been the first person in my family to attend college. Then, I married a surfer-turned-law-student-Orthodox Jew from Hawaii. So, in a way, my first pregnancy was fertile with opportunity for freakishness.

To my surprise, things stayed pretty tame for a while. Every Friday night my husband and I would curl up with the authoritative manual on gestation, *What to Expect When You're Expecting* and read where our babies were "at" that week.[1] Today, you are the size of blueberry. Today, you are the size of raspberry. I thought, *I love blueberries. I even like raspberries. I can do this!* The thought of giving birth to three little blueberries made the whole enterprise seem so unrealistic that it became bearable. We also read an out-of-print book about giving birth to high-order multiples. The women featured in this strange little book had all given birth to triplets, quads, or quintuplets, and it was filled with tips like how to construct a feeding bib and nurse three babies simultaneously in the absence of a third breast. This book encouraged my delusion that triplet mommies were, in fact, completely normal while the quintuplet mommies, well, they were the real carny folk.

* * *

I continued making steady progress in my classes while acting as a greenhouse for the blueberries. One day in my fourteenth week I went to my doctor for a "triplet-routine" nuchal translucency test. Like any good student, I had read up the night before (if you consider WebMD a valid scientific source) and knew what "numbers" I was aiming to score.

But as it turns out, you can't study for this exam. They jostle your abdomen and measure the amount of fluid at the back of each fetus' neck. As the soft-spoken sonographer continued to poke and prod at me for hours, I realized that something was up. She was not shouting out the babies' numbers with triumphant glee. There were no high fives and jubilant smiles. She was sullen and actively silent, as when your advisor reads four weeks of your work without lifting a pen. Then, I heard the inevitable and traumatic, "Let me get the doctor." It turned out two out of my three babies had too much fluid in their little tiny necks. The babies, it would appear, were at the wrong end of the bell curve. They had failed their first test.

Until this life-altering moment, the most serious decision I'd made was what to do with ramen noodles. As I was presented with elimination and reduction options, I remember thinking not about the children but that I was too emotionally immature, too inexperienced in life to handle the weight of this issue. Couldn't I revisit it in ten years? By then, there might be a small chance that I'd be wise enough to make the right decision. I left the office stunned.

Thus far my life had been a series of long-term goals and benchmarks: do well in high school to get into a good college; do well in college to get into a good graduate program; do well in graduate school to get a good job . . . ad infinitum, I guess.

Growing these babies had been the simplest of these responsibilities. And yet, somehow I was failing at it. They needed nothing from me but a relatively healthy diet and an occasional, encouraging pat. This was less than what my career as a graduate student required. Walking out of that appointment, I felt true purposelessness for the first time in my life. I had no function. I had no goal. It was, you could say, a really low day.

* * *

We decided to keep the babies and take our chances. Just like low scorers dismissing the GREs, we waived off the test results. We switched doctors, got a second opinion, and decided that our kids had been underprepared for their test. In solidifying our resolve, this episode shifted how we felt about the pregnancy: clearly, I was not having blueberries.

Besides the nuchal disaster, my pregnancy progressed uneventfully. My new doctor was a specialist who out-schooled my first doctor with an MD and a PhD but didn't take my insurance. As I waded through the red tape to get enrolled on a new plan, I visited the doctor at his clinic in Chinatown. It was like being transplanted every Friday to a little field site in some exotic locale. I began looking forward to my appointments. I liked the Chinese receptionist who typed my medical forms on an old typewriter. I liked handing cash directly to my doctor. And I liked the lack of Manhattan swankiness. In a way, these weekly sojourns became my little side project, an experiment with very real results and findings.

For a while it seemed that my stomach grew in proportion to my graduate workload. I began churning out papers as quickly as I would soon be spouting milk from my breasts. In the springtime, as I grew close to bursting, my husband began carpooling me to campus. I was confined to the back of my parents' car because my mother insisted that our clunker was unreliable for human transport. On the soft leather seats, I would rub my tummy while reviewing for class, usually completing the trip with a solid puking session. Arriving on campus, I would squeeze behind a shrinking wooden desk and spend the next three and half hours feeling like I was wearing my freshman Thanksgiving pants. I started worrying about explaining to babies A and C how baby B got the thick indented mark across her forehead. And worse, I dreaded explaining to her that she got this hideous defect because her mother *just had to* listen to droning lectures on the potential perils of statistical analysis.

Each week, my classmates would clap at the sight of me. *She's still here!* They would cheer the babies on and urge them to *hang in there* and to *let mommy make it* to spring break. Though confident that I would make it through class, I always carried a spare set of underwear just in case. In retrospect, I'm not sure how I thought extra skivvies would be helpful if I suddenly found myself in the ladies' bathroom laboring over the triplets.

As I sat in my desk with my legs tightly crossed, I found myself living two opposing realities: the reality of me as a mother and the reality of me as a wannabe scholar. Initially, these two roles coexisted nicely. I absently rubbed my tummy as I took and passed my qualifying exams; it seemed that my brain and uterus could briefly cohabitate. This feeling was short lived. Toward the end of the pregnancy, I began feeling the weight of carrying these blueberries-turned-watermelons both physically and mentally. *Would being a mom of triplets change the person I was working so hard to become? Would I fail to earn my doctorate and instead be a stay-at-home mom?* This of course was followed by the immediate paranoid follow-up thought: *Was I a self-hating horrible woman for thinking this?* This cycle of crazy took me back to the day I received my first college acceptance letter and the joy of knowing that I would be forging my own path. Starting college, I was simply enthralled by the idea of doing something with my life. In the last stages of my pregnancy, I frequently revisited those early years and considered whether the past few years of my life were ultimately worthless. I mean, they wouldn't help me change diapers even if they did make me a more compassionate and (possibly) hipper mother. The weight of these doubts was my constant companion, along with the crushing force of my ever-exploding bladder.

* * *

One night, while reading the opening paragraph of *Eat, Pray, Love*, I felt a little extra *zoop* on one of my many nocturnal bathroom trips.[2] I returned to bed knowing something was amiss but too tired and humongous to move. Instead, I lay in bed feeling the slight echoing aches. While experiencing labor does not require a college degree, I remained willfully clueless. For weeks I had been inwardly prodded by sixty digits, twelve limbs, and three apple-bobbing heads, so I quickly dismissed the faint rumbling quaking through my core. By morning I finished the book and called my mother: the birth was on.

We drove to the hospital on an early Easter morning. I was only thirty-six weeks along! I imagine that few people in their right mind think of dissertation proposals while preparing to give birth to triplets. But in an odd symptom of nesting syndrome, I had experienced an intense wave of productivity that had led me right to the doorstep of submitting my proposal. Wanting to ride that rare crest to the shoreline, I needed a few more weeks to get it through to my committee. Obviously, the babies had other plans.

As we waited for teams of doctors to show up, I quietly said goodbye to my proposal and shot my advisor a quick e-mail telling her I would finish and send it to her in a month or two. Last words and last laughs, or however the saying goes. As I was wheeled into the OR to Lady Gaga's *Bad Romance*, my mom held my hand tightly. Meanwhile, my husband stood ready at the entrance of the neonatal ICU to meet our babies.

For the long wait and weightiness of the pregnancy, things happened very fast. Baby A was born a perfectly healthy, shrieking little girl. Baby B, her little sister and the runt of the litter, (weighing in at three pounds and twelve ounces) was also born bewildered and indignant. A few long minutes later, baby C rounded out the team with his coconut head and wide boyish nose. With each child's birth, my mother, overjoyed with emotion, burst out Hebrew prayers in which she thanked God for delivering each triplet safely. As we waited between births, I quietly asked my supportive mother to shut up, being more embarrassed by her spirituality than by my publicly splayed insides.

After the babies were whisked away for incubation and further poking, the doctors stitched me up. As they made small talk with my mother and me, they mercifully increased my pain meds. As I slowly drifted away to that happy place, I overheard my mother telling the surgeon about my research; after correcting her (*there is a difference between comic books and graphic narratives, mother!*), I blissfully passed out.

The drug-induced trip seemed to last about four months. The early days are very hazy. Tiny squeaky cries . . . chicken-wing-like hands groping in the darkness . . . mind-numbing exhaustion. I remember feeling fat and needing to desperately brush my hair but never finding that elusive hairbrush or the full five minutes to get it through my thick head-nest. After several weeks, I began catching glimpses of my old, goal-oriented self in the mirror again. Like the researcher I had set out to be, I began organizing my data. I got the babies on a feeding schedule (two, five, eight, and eleven), kept track of their outputs (poops and pee), and measured what they ate. I kept all this information in a thick binder. This ridiculous act somehow made me feel like I was back—that somehow the academic skills I had labored to acquire were actually real life, practical, and world tested. I kept this binder with me always, and in that first year, it reminded me to keep to the path I had started on long ago.

* * *

When the triplets turned one, I returned to graduate school full time, determined to complete my doctoral degree. I not only began my dissertation but also started teaching on campus and participating in research. Some days, I would change forty diapers and then grade forty papers. Resuming my full student duties was difficult. I think people were secretly surprised to see me. Grad school is a committed lifestyle, and once you are out of it, it can be very difficult to remember how things work. It's also very hard to reconvince yourself that spending boatloads of money and fighting with an uninspiring computer are worthy of your attention and time. When I initially went back to work, I gave myself all sorts of pep talks: *People want to know this research! It's groundbreaking! Graphic novels are the future!* Oh wait, we're out of milk.

My life had changed so much so quickly, but graduate school was just how I'd left it. The outdated research poster was still up, and the Mr. Coffee machine in the lounge was still there, still broken. Walking down the still monotonous hallways, talking to the same people doing the same thing, I felt like Hindi's clone revisiting her old life. Getting back into the groove, I tried to be the person I was before I'd had my kids. I felt the inexplicable need to prove my graduate student-ness. I talked too much at research meetings, e-mailed my advisor too many times, and occasionally hung around the broken Mr. Coffee for no apparent reason.

While I was working hard to deflect attention from the formula stain on my shirt and the fact that I now drove a minivan, others perceived me differently. Everyone in my department now knew me as "the student with the triplets." So I was odd—nothing new. But this oddness became an unfortunate issue the day I told my advisor that I was looking for an academic position. Thoughtfully, she reminded me that I had young children at home and such a position might be too demanding for my current "state." Since when did being a mother become a career handicap? A quick Google search of the term "academic mothers" revealed the sad truth: we women are far less likely than our nonbreeding counterparts to secure a tenure track position. This discovery was heartbreaking. I felt disappointed, disillusioned, and totally confounded.

Many of the people I worked with on a daily basis had children. And though they were not openly hostile to the idea of offspring, they didn't actively endorse them either. People were pleasant and professional but did not express the slightest interest or compassion for my mushy, wet, and sticky life. No one offered any real advice or practical guidance on how to remain both a serious mother and a serious academic without compromising the integrity of either role.

Though I don't think that this sense of dislocation was the result of a department-wide conspiracy, it did give me the opportunity to consider my own new enormous responsibilities and long-held personal goals. Without the faintest clue about how to reconcile these opposing roles, I became a self-induced schizophrenic. During my long drives to campus, I warped into my "academic self" by listening to NPR and sipping Starbucks. I limited my home talk and blamed kid-related emergencies on the weather or traffic. In pretending I was not a mother, I basically tried, fruitlessly I might add, to reestablish myself as a normal person, to go to department events and attend conferences, without the "baggage" of three infant children. On the way home, I morphed back into "mom," throwing my hair up in a ponytail and swinging by the pharmacy for the latest carload of diapers. Though this went on for almost six months, the entire time I felt miserable, guilty even, and as if each "self" was somehow cheating on the other.

* * *

Eventually, I began realizing that acting like a double agent was the real problem. Becoming a mother fundamentally changed me. It changed the way I thought. It changed the way I dealt with people. It even changed the way I dressed. There was no way to amputate the "mother" from the "academic" me; it was fused with the rest of the hot mess of my life and identity. So I gave up trying to keep my identities separate. I got dressed for work as a mom. I brushed my hair and teeth as a mom. And I mashed potatoes for dinner as a graduate student. I was unabashedly myself, allowing all the complex spheres of my life to orbit simultaneously. Side by side, I put my books on toilet training next to my research collection. No explosions occurred. Nothing dramatic happened. I wasn't thrown out of school. The diapers and the dissertation could coexist. Each enhanced the other by adding a layer of complexity. With a restored sense of self, I continued forward, determined to scale the behemoth brick wall that is the dissertation.

In many ways, my experience in writing the dissertation wasn't unlike raising a particularly petulant and precocious progeny. It was needy. It was demanding. It sucked up all my energy, time, and at moments, even my will to live. But like any especially annoying child, it was also a source of incredible joy. This is because, like it or not, my dissertation was me. Like a toilet-training toddler who just wet her pants for the umpteenth time, my dissertation was my baby; it was my academic personality and intellectual DNA reflected on paper. And sometimes it got stinky, but I loved it anyways.

Though I had a restored sense of self, I still struggled to balance the demands of writing with my three-ring-circus home life. Everything was an excuse to ignore the pile of data waiting to be sorted and analyzed. First, I couldn't find time to work. So we hired a nanny. Then, I couldn't find a place to work. So, I bought a neat little folding table and set it up in the one room we had. It took weeks before I actually sat down to face my computer screen. I sifted through the papers. Then, I went to find my lucky pen. Then, I desperately needed to do laundry. After all this, I still found myself with time to blink. As I shifted the pile of papers to a better location, I was suddenly bombarded by thoughts of all the things I could be doing with these quiet, naptime hours. Though the daily excuses differed, many weeks passed before I wrote a single word.

My commute to campus became an opportunity to conduct little pep rallies. *I am starting it today! I will write the first page today! I will at least write the first word today!* Then, I'd return home, exhilarated from teaching and exhausted from life and wonder how three monkeys had managed to escape from the zoo and why they were destroying my tiny Brooklyn apartment. One night as I sat down to work I looked at my son Ezra in his crib and, instead of writing, began wondering what he was thinking and why he was giving me the stink eye. Or wait, maybe he needs glasses! This inevitably landed me in a Wikipedia-induced coma—another writing opportunity lost, never to return.

* * *

My mother was the first to mention the J–O–B and our need of a real part-time second income, not the grad student pittance that barely covered gas and tolls. At family dinners, she would seize her chest and cry, "Tell me, are you going to graduate with your children?" My parents, much like my colleagues, had assumed that the birth of the triplets had signaled the demise of my academic career. Joyful over their adorable grandchildren, they had been prepared to rip my piles of data and sit *shiva* for it. In their minds, where one began, the other ended. They just couldn't believe that I still gave a damn about the use of diegetic space in comics when I had three children to raise.

This clash was undoubtedly a result of both generational differences and cultural expectations. Growing up, I found a fresh snack waiting on the table every day after school. Each night, we set the table, had a bowl of soup, and ate a protein, starch, and a vegetable. My children, in contrast, were able to double fist two slices of pizza right out of the box by the age of two. No plate or table was required, just a small patch of grass amidst the Brooklyn pavement. My mom's parenting style was calculated, organized, and perfect; mine is chaotic, desperate, and *meshuga*.

As I worked to finish the Big D, I moved my gear into my parents' basement in hopes that the location change would help me focus and finally finish it. Most of the time, this was a stellar arrangement; I would put the kids to bed and then escape into the night. Occasionally, when I was in the throes of some deep insight, my mother felt it was her sacred duty to interrupt and remind me that I had children at home. She did this in bizarre but creative ways:

"Look at these adorable pink pants I picked up from Children's Place."

"Cute."

"You know, you'd think these pants could match any kind of top, but I went to four stores and couldn't match them with anything. Do the girls have anything to go with this?"

[Grunt] "Dunno."

"Can you look up please? You know the dissertation isn't going away, but the girls need pink pants for the summer."

"Okay. I guess they could go with a black or white top." (This is my match-all excuse for all clothes.)

"That would look ridiculous. Why do I even ask you?"

[Grunt] "Dunno."

I continued plugging onward. The dissertation became my Rubik's cube, my Shangri-la, my Everest, and I became obsessed with completing it. I had found an exciting academic position starting the following fall and was working on a major publication for the summer. For the first time since starting graduate school, I felt like my academic life was on the cusp of emerging. I thought about the fancy restaurant I would eat at after my defense and the professorial jacket I would buy to go with my new academic position.

* * *

But then there was my advisor's tepid review of my first draft, and I came crashing back to Earth. Suddenly there was laundry everywhere. The dishes in the sink were emitting unnatural odors. Had we really been eating cereal and peanut butter sandwiches for a month? Also, I couldn't help but notice that my children had emerged as people: Ellie roamed around the house roaring like a "tiger cat," Judy had "why" syndrome, and Ezra only wanted to play Japanese word games on the computer.

They were also escape artists, imprisoned baby ninjas refusing to nap. I'd put them down only to see two pairs of raccoon eyes reflecting in the computer screen within minutes. The third ninja, too intelligent for crib acrobatics, would scream, "Poop! I poop!" Running to change her diaper, I would find her not only clean as a whistle but also giggling with glee. One night, it suddenly hit me that their "room" had no doors; in fact, there was no room, since their cribs were hunkered down in the vaguely defined "living space" of our small apartment. Coaxing our kids to bed each night with bribes of ice cream and Elmo was getting old. It was time for me to graduate so we could start our lives.

So the Big D still isn't done. Though it's taken a long time, I'm finally learning to balance the disparate components of my world. I try to keep sight of the big picture. During the last Skype call with my advisor, Ezra managed to escape from his crib and sneak up behind me. My advisor noticed him there before I did. Though it was disconcerting to see his drooling face while heatedly discussing APA headings, I just shrugged.

At this moment, Ezra is jumping in his crib singing "ice cream truck song"; Judy is eating pasta right out of the fridge; and Ellie is coloring the walls with a pink crayon. I glance up from my computer, smile, and get back to work. These days the twin narratives of motherhood and academia have become wonderfully intertwined and thoroughly codependent. In other words, I embrace the crazy and don't try to fight it anymore.

NOTES

1. Heidi Murkoff and Sharon Mazel, *What to Expect When You're Expecting* (New York: Workman Press, 2008).

2. Elizabeth Gilbert, *Eat, Pray, Love: One Woman's Search for Everything across Italy, India, and Indonesia* (New York: Viking, 2007).

12

WHO'S PRO-CREATING NOW?

Two Sides of Parenting in the Academe

Lara Narcisi and Scott Dimovitz

A MOTHER'S PERSPECTIVE: LARA NARCISI

When I told the dean I wouldn't be requesting any maternity leave, he gave me a high five. And thus I received what any untenured woman wants: validation that she is not going to be a problem and that no one made a mistake in hiring her or, for that matter, in accepting her entire gender into the vaunted ranks of the academe. Thus, after I had my first son, I went right back to work when the semester began, two and a half weeks later.

As the writing director, I was running part of first-year orientation, so on my first day back I drove an hour across town to drop my baby off with my mother and returned just in time to make a brief speech welcoming the entire incoming class. It was shortly thereafter, as I was standing in front of my own group of advisees for the first time, that I noticed the two symmetrical circles of breast milk that had successfully penetrated the mama armor of my bra, breast pads, and summer-thin shirt. This proved to be an apt indicator of my attempts to balance the personal and the professional: messy.

* * *

My professor/mother path began when, against everyone's advice including my own, I fell in love with someone in my graduate school. Dual hires are nearly impossible, especially for humanities professors seeking small liberal arts colleges, but the fact that we were in the same graduate program, studying the same time period, and sporting very similar credentials made us doubt the possibility of achieving jobs in the same time zone, let alone the same school. So began our long-distance affair. Many of our colleagues have similar stories: transcontinental commutes lasting for half a decade or more; the high cost and low satisfaction of two different households; and a desperate reliance on the early versions of Skype that made us appear to be transmitting our images from the moon.

Scott and I applied for some one hundred jobs—*each*—for five consecutive years, which became an extremely unexciting side business involving an epic amount of faxing. We published, polished our pedagogy, and participated in every possible campus committee at our respective institutions. And then there was a certain moment where diligence ceased and luck interceded, because somehow, miraculously, we both obtained tenure-track jobs at our dream school: a small liberal arts college in Denver (my hometown, no less!), with a strong emphasis on values and ethics and the warmest, most dedicated English department we could imagine.

Perhaps it was something in the mountain air, but everyone else on campus seemed to appreciate their good fortune as well. The students loved the department so much that they started an English club, set up a highly trafficked and geekery-laden Facebook page, created trivia and dodgeball teams (the latter less successful than the former), and started a small cottage industry making literary T-shirts. We were inspired by all this student energy and by the genuine bonhomie of our colleagues, and all the struggles that had led up to this moment seemed absolutely worth it.

Cue the progeny. Like many of my female colleagues, I was aiming for a May baby in order to minimize the impact on my professional responsibilities.[1] While my friend Cath nailed it by birthing just days after graduation, my son missed the memo and chose to arrive at the end of the summer. So he was three months late by my academic clock and of course years late by my biological one.

Was this good timing? There is probably no such thing for a mother-professor, so I'll avoid proffering any advice on that score.[2] "Family planning" is a luxury we aren't technically supposed to partake of at a

Catholic school,³ but I personally opted to wait in order to avoid long-distance parenting.

Once pregnant, I found myself grateful that my morning sickness was, like me, a night owl and struck only in the evenings, so I never actually vomited during a class—although my students' well-intentioned multicultural potluck feast, including fried samosas, chile con carne, and a particularly redolent gumbo, proved a close call. The English majors were exuberant on our behalf, offering entries for our "Pick the Baby's Literary Name" contest that ranged from the plausible (Atticus, Emerson) to the laughable (Queequeg, Dracula). Colleagues gave us books like *My First Poetry Compendium* and *Chaucer for Toddlers* and onesies proclaiming their literary heritage by inquiring "Is this a diaper I see before me?" or "Shall I disturb the universe?"

Despite all the goodwill, I knew that I had progressed from cute pregnant to gross pregnant when an older male colleague puffed out his cheeks and did an exaggeratedly unflattering imitation of my duck waddle to the snickers of our passing students. Teaching while rotund wasn't fun the first time, but given my aging ovaries I did it again in rapid succession. As any working mother of two could attest, fetuses can't wreak nearly the havoc on your professional life that they can once born.

During both of my initial semesters back postpartum, I felt my energetic classroom style slow to the pace of my sons' crawl; my speech often seemed no more intelligible than theirs. Attempting to write anything with a thesis more advanced than "how to remove spit-up in three easy steps" seemed a Herculean effort. I found myself hoping that my literary theory students were taking my incomplete sentences as some sort of intentional Derridean commentary on the inherent instability of linguistic communication rather than the derogatorily termed "mommy brain." Being a working mother is inevitably a precarious balancing act that probably requires a career on autopilot. If your job is being a professional thinker, however, there is no such escape, and unfortunately being procreative tends to render one anticreative.⁴

I thought often of Grace Paley, who wrote in her 1959 semiautobiographical "Two Short Sad Stories from a Long and Happy Life," "I have raised these kids, with one hand typing behind my back to earn a living."⁵ I always picture Paley stretching her myriad limbs, octopus-like, as she attempts to work and simultaneously wrangle a wayward toddler.

In order to leave my own right hand free for typing, I nursed my baby almost exclusively on my left side. I ended up both looking and feeling like a one-breasted Amazonian warrior.

Despite the struggles, neither my husband nor I wanted to change our careers or parenting. Now that we had finally found this wonderful school and were so happily in possession of two adorable, pudgy, literarily named little replicas of ourselves, who were we to miss a meeting or a class because of a sick infant? Rather than complain, we decided to attempt the 1960s Superwoman archetype, boldly pursuing both career and family and forgoing both recreation and sleep.

Without enough money to spare for full-time child care, the only choice was to perfect a challenging juggling act. We scheduled our classes so we could do a high-speed baby-stroller toss-off in the hallways during passing periods; we read James Joyce assignments aloud to our sons instead of singing to them; and we attempted to smuggle the kids into the back of the faculty senate and hoped no one would notice the crying contraband. Our schedules were and still are coordinated to the minute—like super-spies, minus the glamor.

Is this crazy? A bit. Is it practical or even possible for most couples, even when both are in academia? No. Does it always work? Of course not. There are days when both of us absolutely have to finish a syllabus or an article and both children are screaming, and we end up modeling some stellar parenting techniques like locking our older son in his playroom and letting the baby cry in his swing while we cover our ears and speed-type.

When our toddler chooses not to nap, which is often, our entire work schedules are thrown off, and one of us usually ends up driving in circles around the neighborhood until he finally conks out in the car and we frantically attempt to complete our reading for the next day in the parking lot of a nearby supermarket. I have read entire novels in five-minute segments—not exactly conducive to analytical thought.

When both parents are exhausted from teaching all day, there isn't much refuge if the children decide to engage in an impromptu screaming concert or if one opts to color the walls with a Sharpie while the other selects spit-up finger paint as his artistic medium. We do this, though, because equality matters to us, profoundly. My husband is the only man on our Women and Gender Studies committee; he teaches courses on feminism, he believes in it deeply, and he chooses to live his beliefs. When I discuss national gender pay inequities in my courses, I can honestly say that for us at least this is not the case, because my husband and I earn the same salary to the penny. I also love that for about a year our older son would mix us up, referring to either of us as "Mommy" or "Daddy" interchangeably, or occasionally opting for the single unit, "Mommydaddy." Equality both at home and at work is the most difficult balance; having one partner as a wage earner and the other as a homemaker is unquestionably simpler and probably easier. But we have devoted the time and effort to making the balance work, and thus far it is working—for us, for our school, and for both of our sons.

There are certainly days when I think the idea that I can combine my two worlds is merely a delusion of the permanently sleep deprived, that I'll never publish again and that my children will grow up hating not only me but also all of literature for seemingly displacing them in my affections. Most often, though, I like to think my understanding of literature has deepened because I'm a mother and that I'm a better mother because I've already practiced on hundreds of students.

A FATHER'S PERSPECTIVE: SCOTT DIMOVITZ

I grew up in the hazy, scrim-covered lens of the 1970s, a world where feminism was a given to my child's worldview and not a contested "perspective." Boys and girls of all colors were represented on *Sesame Street*. Alan Alda cried in therapy in a very special episode of $M^*A^*S^*H$.

Every year (sometimes twice) throughout elementary school, a burnt-out teacher would play Marlo Thomas's feminist musical special *Free to Be . . . You and Me* on a decommissioned government projector, and through instantly catchy folk songs I internalized a world where men and women were absolutely equal in all things: Alan Alda and Marlo Thomas voiced a version of Atalanta, where I learned that a young woman could choose her own mate, if she even wanted to get married; in "William Wants a Doll," a boy could like sports and still want to change a baby; and a gigantic Rosie Grier assured me that "It's All Right to Cry" because "crying gets the sad out of you."

Add to this general cultural background of equality a guilt-filled Catholic upbringing and a father whose primary achievement as a parent was serving as a model of what not to do, and I was a potpourri of male guilt, wanting nothing more than to make up for the sins of the institutional and personal father by not visiting that punishment on my own sons. I wanted a career that would allow me to be present in the upbringing and primary care of my kids.

Being a college professor seemed perfect, providing intellectual stimulation by helping the next generation develop to their highest potential by exposing them to great literature and helping them to become critical thinkers, while still allowing me to be an integral part of my children's lives. I could teach regular courses on feminist literature and return home to see how my dedication to the cause translated in the home. And there was no way my kids would get the thousand-yard stare every time Harry Chapin's "Cat's in the Cradle" came on the radio.

When my wife and I met in graduate school, our shared passions, values, and goals trumped our radically different backgrounds, even while we knew it was ridiculous to fall in love with another academic—especially another English literature academic. As Lara already mentioned, the dual academic hire was a farcical Atlantis for graduate students. Five years on the job market and we finally landed in not only the same school but also the same department, a preposterous violation of probability that still surprises us every day. We married immediately and began the junior academics' push for delayed procreation.

Meanwhile, as a spousal hire, I felt I had to prove myself very quickly, and I worked on publishing, pedagogy, and committee work in equal measure. Our three-quarter loads, teaching upward of three new preps every semester for the first three years, left little time for anything but our careers, and we joked that we married not only each other but our school as well.

Dinners consisted of talking about shared students and prep for the next day, occasionally mixing up a student's name with one of the dishes we were eating, and evenings we read into the night, taking only occasional breaks to watch highbrow relaxation episodes of *The Wire* or reruns of *Northern Exposure*.

My wife was pregnant with our first son by the end of my first semester teaching. I announced to friends and family that "we" were pregnant, until that was teased out of me by the purportedly progressive men around me, who asked how long it took after I had sprouted a uterus before I was "with child." After watching my wife going through night sickness and almost passing out in public three times a day, I conceded their point, even though I was committed to being there for her. I half jokingly referred to having "womb envy" and wished I could be more intimately part of the process beyond the initial contribution. Biology trumped ideology, but I could still do what I could. I read books, as I always encounter reality, and attended classes with my wife at the local hospital on the birthing process, proper nursing techniques, and diapering. I also took a men-only class called "A Boot Camp for New Dads"—an embarrassingly macho take on gender roles in which the instructor wore camouflage shorts and a whistle, and the khaki-colored materials sported an army stencil aesthetic. Once we got past the pastel reenactment of the first half of *Full Metal Jacket* and the long lecture about how we shouldn't shake our babies—apparently a large problem where we live—the class surprised me as it was largely composed of professional men in their thirties who shared a number of anxieties. Would we be able to "provide"— defined not exclusively in a 1950s version of money but in terms of empathy, warmth, and time? If we had some momentary lapse in parenting judgment, how long would the trauma last? Would we repeat the mistakes of our fathers? Would we break our children?

When our son was born, I thought about that class often. I quickly realized something that had never been developed in all of those years of feminist upbringing: no one really cares about the new dad. Not that I thought that I was going through something *more difficult* than my wife—it wasn't a competition, after all—but that, even in the academy, men had no support network in place to talk about what parenting was like and what challenges come up, while trying to juggle the demands of a pretenured life with kids.

My wife had her mother and her best friend, who was going through the same experience at almost the exact same time. Most of my close male friends were back on the East Coast, and none of them were raising kids. Many of our young colleagues were female academics who had waited to have children as had my wife, and they quickly disseminated—along with the boxes of used baby clothing and toys—all manner of advice and commiseration.

Most of the male faculty were older than I was and had grown children, whose upbringing faded into some fond memory of difficult yet rewarding times, usually with their wives doing most of the legwork. A local group of new moms in our neighborhood in Denver had organized a highly structured support network called the Highland Mommies, where professional women who had given up their careers or were taking time off met regularly with other mothers of similarly aged children to talk about parenting issues and resources. There is no Highland Daddies.

For a previous generation of men, even for the most progressive among them, this just wouldn't be an issue; either the sexual division of labor would have the mother staying home (as did both my wife's mother and my mother), or women who wanted a career would find a daycare center as soon as possible (as several of our colleagues did). A father who coparented day to day just wasn't that common, and it seemed irrelevant in our culture, forty years after *Free to Be . . . You and Me*.

Everyone asked how my wife was doing, and rightfully so. Nothing is easy for any mothers, college professors or not. As far as we've come, there are still not enough resources in place to support new parents. But almost no one asked how I was, even though I felt as if I was barely getting by. I realized quickly that I had no idea what I was doing. While Marlo Thomas assured me that William could have a doll, I had played with *Star Wars* action figures. I had never even held a baby, much less changed a diaper, warmed up a bottle of frozen breast milk, or learned how to have a baby "cry it out" at nap time. Books helped a little, but the fuzzy ideology of most contemporary child-rearing books refused any prescriptive ideas. Just go with the flow.

Of course, the more I felt these issues, the guiltier I felt. My wife was the one breast-feeding, after all, and she had just gone through that funhouse mirror of physical and emotional stress that was pregnancy and childbirth. I taught Feminist Literature, for heaven's sake, where we deconstructed Coventry Patmore's nineteenth-century Victorian ideas of women being the "angel of the house" and mocked clips from *Leave It to Beaver* and *Father Knows Best*. I felt the weight of several millennia of patriarchal oppression, so who was I, as a man, to be stressed out, going into my second year teaching, trying to keep publishing on a three-quarter load?

My wife and I juggled the joys of new parenthood from those early days with the inevitable stress of a new career, and as the years went on and a second son joined the first, we got better at finding a kind of balance. From the beginning, we were both committed to doing 50 percent of the child rearing, yet we quickly realized that two professors working full time doesn't feel as much like 50 percent + 50 percent but more like 100 percent + 100 percent.

In the first few years, we used no child care, aside from one weekly visit to grandma's, but since then we have worked out an intricate system of trade-offs and occasional babysitters. We've gotten better at the timing over time, and we have come to accept that no perfect parenting is possible, which would sound like one of those parenting guides' fuzzy clichés if it weren't such a complex negotiation of joy, responsibility, and guilt.

I finish this writing on a Saturday morning in a coffee shop across from my wife, who is grading papers for her William Faulkner class, while we pay a babysitter ten dollars an hour for the privilege. Hopefully, our children's first memories won't be of felt abandonment because of this moment—that we chose a few hours pursuing our profession over another round of "The Wheels on the Bus." Hopefully, Freud was wrong, and we can all outlive the sins of the parents.

NOTES

1. On this topic, see Carmen Armenti, "May Babies and Posttenure Babies: Maternal Decisions of Women Professors," *Review of Higher Education* 27, no. 2 (winter 2004): 211–31.

2. Others don't, though. Kathryn Lynch, in her June 7, 2002, commentary in *The Chronicle of Higher Education*, "An Immodest Proposal: Have Children in Graduate School," recommends graduate school as the ideal time to procreate (sleeplessness is great for dissertation writing). And in their 2011 book *Professor Mommy* (Lanham, MD: Rowman & Littlefield), Bowdoin professor/mothers Rachel Connelly and Kristen Ghodsee recommend avoiding the time during tenure track if possible (forty-five is the new twenty-five for childbearing). However, in her March 10, 1995, article in *The Chronicle of Higher Education*, "Scheduling Motherhood," Robin Wilson profiles professors who have had children at various different career stages; all found it difficult, and several, particularly those with heavy research demands, relinquished either academic aspirations or the prospect of parenthood (okay, women can't have it all).

3. Although a 2010 report by the Guttmacher Institute reported that 99 percent of women use contraception at some point over their lifetimes (http://www.guttmacher.org/pubs/fb_contr_use.html), in 2012 the president for the Association of Catholic Colleges and Universities, Michael Galligan-Stierle, recommended that women so radical as to want contraception should avoid attending Catholic institutions, just as "no one would go to a Jewish barbecue and expect pork chops to be served" (reported by Denise Grady for the *New York Times* in "Ruling on Contraception Draws Battle Lines at Catholic Colleges," January 29, 2012, http://www.nytimes.com/2012/01/30/health/policy/law-fuels-contraception-controversy-on-catholic-campuses.html?pagewanted=all&_r=0). My ovaries and I don't want thirteen children but do love our Catholic college.

4. This, of course, doesn't stop everyone from telling us how easy we have it, what with those luxurious summers "off" and all. For example, in her August 2012 cover article for *The Atlantic*, "Why Women Still Can't Have It All," Anne-Marie Slaughter states that an academic career can be ideal for mothers, because unlike her political career, it allows for flexible work hours. Unfortunately, those flexible hours have a tendency to become *all* hours.

5. Grace Paley, "Two Short Sad Stories from a Long and Happy Life," in *The Little Disturbances of Man: Stories of Women and Men at Love*, 127–46 (New York: Penguin, 1959).

13

HOW I GOT DISMISSED FROM JURY DUTY
A Reflection on Philosophy and Public Life

Rick Anthony Furtak

Teachers of philosophy often refer to themselves simply as "philosophers," as evidenced by the title of a newsletter that circulates within the discipline called *Jobs for Philosophers*. Although no joke is intended, this phrase captures the ironic juxtaposition of lofty aspirations alongside the utterly mundane business of looking for academic employment.

What could be a more noble pursuit than philosophical reflection? Yet what could be so ridiculous as the prospect of scanning every item on a list of positions for assistant professors, while knowing that your livelihood depended on it? But after I *did* get one of those jobs for philosophers, it became my everyday business to be teaching and writing about exalted philosophical ideas.

So when I introduced myself in the courtroom one summer when I was still just a few years out of graduate school and preparing to teach my fall semester courses, I probably used the term "philosopher" in one way or another. Was I making an issue of it, daring anyone to laugh as if that sounded even a bit odd? Or did I want to show that my profession wasn't just some drudgery from which I escaped as soon as possible, yelling in joy like Fred Flintstone when I heard the five o'clock whistle?

When the judge asked what activities I enjoyed on my own time, I answered that much of my time was devoted to reading, writing, thinking, and talking about ideas. As the judge began to smile ever so subtly,

I realized that I'd better not leave it at that but should say more in reply to the standard questions about job and hobbies. Otherwise it would be as if I had introduced myself by saying, "I'm a knight," only to follow that up by adding that what I enjoy is performing feats of knight errantry. Fortunately, before he moved on to the next potential juror, I had time to say that I was also an avid baseball fan, thus locating myself back on Planet Earth along with my fellow citizens there in the courtroom.

As others were being interviewed, I tried not to let it bother me that the judge seemed to be judging me, making the very same assumption as the stranger on the train who had asked, "Are you reading that book for a class assignment?" And I had wanted to say, "Well, no, it's not for a class! I actually like reading this kind of thing, damn it! If I put up with *some* amount of stupid bullshit in my line of work, it's only so that I can spend large amounts of time with books and ideas, and actually earn my bread in a way that's related to what I enjoy doing, what I love reading, writing, and thinking about!" Unfortunately, I actually hadn't prepared this answer until I got to the courthouse, not that it would have been well received there either.

But ever since arriving at the station beside the courthouse, I had been blending in pretty well. The aforementioned book was stashed away in my little bag, and I was casually dressed even to the point of wearing shorts. I had done nothing since entering the courtroom to give the impression that I was an intellectual with his head in the clouds. And I'm fairly certain that no one knew about my drifting into the nearby U.S. Mint building while looking for the courthouse, where I nearly stumbled into a tour showing how coins are made. Now, like the rest of them, I was here doing my part to serve, or to show myself worthy of serving, my civic duty.

As we quickly found out, it was going to be a murder trial—although, as the judge also assured us right away, it was not one for which the death penalty would be applicable. This made me, and everyone else as far as I could tell, only slightly relieved. It was serious business in which we might be involved if we were chosen, no doubt—and it was clear before the judge finished asking us his initial round of questions that everyone was rising to the occasion. No matter what anyone had felt earlier that morning about the prospect of spending a week or more on jury duty, there was a palpable sense sweeping over us—I kid you not— that each of us *wanted* to do this, that we wanted to be selected, to prove ourselves worthy, and to rearrange our schedule as drastically as necessary, *anything* to be picked by the team captain! To some degree, I was getting caught up in it myself.

The words "murder trial" made me abandon my plan to take my book out again during the dull moments, and I was now as attentive and engaged as anyone. I didn't want to be set apart from the others, or to be told that I was unfit to participate, even though I had probably already jeopardized my candidacy. I tried to stop gritting my teeth and "put on my good behavior," as my grade school teachers used to say.

Yet as the judge finished his last questions and I heard other people relating their neatly separated jobs and hobbies (accountant and rock climber, nurse's assistant and musician), I wanted to jump to my feet and cry out, "Don't you see? I'm not the oddball here! Doesn't everyone want to spend most of their time doing what they love? And if what you most love to do occupies only a few hours per week—taking the boat out on Sunday afternoon, or whatever—then isn't it a pity to give the rest of your waking life to a job that is nothing more than an unpleasant necessity?"

Call me greedy, but I wouldn't be happy with that arrangement. After delivering more than my share of pizzas and newspapers, and working one summer emptying slot machines (back in the day when they were filled with metal tokens), I know what it's like to work long hours at a job, or even a couple of jobs, that prevent you from having enough time to do what feels like your real purpose in life. And when *that* gets pushed into the margins, then you're forced to spend the rest of your time playing the lead role in a philosophical drama called "The Viciously Circular Argument." It goes like this: you work in order to earn the means of remaining alive, and you remain alive in order to keep working that same job. You're like the drunkard who appears in *The Little Prince*, drinking only to forget that he is ashamed, yet he is ashamed just because he drinks![1] His problem is not his alcoholism per se but the way he keeps on going around in a circle, doing everything for the sake of something else, in an endless sequence that has no meaning: no love, all need. In short, his life is absurd.

But back to the courtroom: paying attention, yes! So I was trying to be attentive. And now it was time for the two lawyers to interrogate us and eliminate those who would be excused. Each lawyer—the prosecution and the defense—could dismiss a certain number of us voluntarily, without having to give an explanation. Right away it was evident that they only had a few genuine questions; the rest of the "questions" took the form of rhetorical slogans of the kind that a salesman might ask. For example, "If I show that the defendant is guilty, then will you deliver a guilty verdict?" Or, from the other side: "If they fail to convict him on every count, will you vote for an acquittal?" *What utter crap*, I thought (well, I thought worse). Just as this random sampling of American citizens was behaving more responsibly and intelligently than ever before, we were being talked at like idiots.

After a few more repetitions of the same rhetorical questions, some groans began to be heard among the potential jurors. It's always good when someone says what everyone is thinking, and the man who was sitting next to me—after hearing the *exact same* question asked to one of us after another—leaned over and whispered, "What shit!" Yes it was, and I nodded in agreement, shrugging as I said quietly, or so I thought, "They must feel as if they have to do this, for some unknown reason," although God knows what it was. Seeing which of us would be the least irritated by leading questions? Or which would yield most easily to their influence?

Did they have to do this? Was *this* part of their job? These questions brought me back to the topic of my own line of work. Admittedly, not every occupational moment would qualify as something I would happily do if I were independently wealthy and free to do *whatever* I wanted. Maybe I was protesting too much on behalf of what it was *supposed* to be like. Although my career *might* give me the opportunity to spend many of my working hours doing what I loved to do, it is not always so rewarding. Indeed, the eerie atmosphere of pointlessness that had descended onto the courtroom was not unfamiliar.

As I resisted slipping into a nightmarish daydream about the many tedious meetings of academic life, it occurred to me that I could cite my own expertise in existential philosophy as a reason for departing from any situations that I judged to be objectively absurd. And I *almost* laughed, although I should have been crying about how the buzz of chatter and gossip that goes on in an academic discipline can sometimes threaten to drown out what matters most.[2] If it gets so bad that you lose sight of what brought you into this in the first place, then your life in the academy can seem as if it's filled with precisely the kind of absurdity you were trying to avoid by not going to law school.

After this train of thought, I began to look at the lawyers with a little more sympathy. One of them was finally asking a more specific question to a potential juror who had a career in (and perhaps a passion for) nonviolent conflict resolution. The lawyer asked what he thought when he heard the word "gangs." Being remarkably diplomatic, maybe because he wanted to get picked for the team, he replied that it made him think of community. I felt a renewed solidarity with the rest of the would-be jurors and a determination to perform my civic duty as capably as anyone could. But, alas! A few moments later I would find myself reciting a cynical saying, about what frequently happens to good intentions, as I walked out of the room. But it wasn't my fault! Not entirely.

I'd heard that no one who admits to doing philosophy for a living makes the cut in jury selection. I think it's because the rest of the world finds us too annoying, though I've been told that it's actually because the lawyers think that we'll exert a disproportionate influence on the deliberations when it's time to render a verdict. Really? Or is it because they assume we might subscribe to a crazy theory of some kind, along the lines of "everyone is innocent" or "everyone is guilty," either of which would constitute a clear bias in any trial? I didn't believe anything as crazy as *that*, did I? When one of the lawyers asked if it's possible to make a *judgment* in an instant, I felt like piping up and saying that, not only did I agree that this was possible, but also I had even committed myself in print to the theoretical view that judgments could be made very quickly!

Here's how it went: The lawyer said, "The other day I was driving,"—false first-person story, I thought, an obvious huckster's tactic—"and I came to a light that was just turning from yellow to red." Oh, *did* he? (Maybe he said it was from green to yellow, since I don't suppose he would admit to breaking the law.) He continued by adding, "I judged that I could safely go through before the light changed." Yes! He was right: it was a judgment, albeit a quick one! I was so excited to voice my agreement that I could barely contain myself. So, to make a long story short, I didn't . . . contain myself, that is. Not only did I feel like chiming in, but also I *did* chime in. I raised my hand for the sake of the greater good and probably confirmed the worst of stereotypes about philosophers. "Yes, that *is* a judgment!" I exclaimed, "but not a *deliberate* judgment." The judge jumped in at that point, cutting me off and noting for the record that the term "deliberate" was not in the legal definition that was at issue. Fair enough. Yet did this need to be so embarrassing? Did it have to count as "the last straw" as far as my competence, or good behavior, was concerned?

As it turns out, yes. There appeared to be a growing sense among the courtroom authorities who were present that my role in this process was not entirely helpful and that it was in the interest of the public good *not* for me to open my mouth again. In fact, my fellow citizens had just been warned against listening to me at all! And it's true, I had already been "reprimanded for talking with my neighbor during class," as they say, prompting a dirty look from the other lawyer. (The same "neighbor" also remarked to me that, if the defendant was guilty of anything, it might only have been "of being in the wrong place at the wrong time," and this also made me laugh.)

Since there was no place for me here as teacher, or teacher's pet, or teammate, or even conversation partner, I was left with only one option: to settle into the role of the rude and outspoken smartass. This was a familiar role, although I thought I had abandoned it many years before grad school. From that point on, I didn't even try to look innocent and polite. Before they finished the questions, I would be caught whispering and snickering once again. And as soon as it was time for the "voluntary" dismissals to be made, I was the very first one to receive this dubious honor.

As they called my name, I rose from my seat and began walking out, feeling slightly self-conscious about having decided to wear shorts. My first thought was, *What a shame, since I've already taken an interest in this trial, and I would have done my best to make sure that we all arrived at the right judgment.* As I entered the hallway, my second thought was, *Maybe it's just as well.* After all, I was ready to reach into my bag for that book I had hidden away. I'd been neglecting other life-and-death matters for too long already.

NOTES

1. Antoine de Saint-Exupéry, *The Little Prince*, trans. Richard Howard (Orlando: Harcourt, 2000), 34–36.

2. An especially moving lamentation of this risk is James McKelly's essay "Life and Death and the American Graduate Student," *Midwest Quarterly* 32 (1990): 112–27. It provides a painful account of the academic processes that threaten to destroy "that fragile, trusting part of ourselves" that made us want to pursue a life of the mind.

ABOUT THE EDITORS AND CONTRIBUTORS

EDITORS

Erin Marie Furtak is associate professor of education at the University of Colorado at Boulder. She earned degrees in biology (BA, University of Colorado), education (MA, University of Denver), and curriculum and teacher education (PhD, Stanford University) before embarking on her German postdoc/adventure at the Max Planck Institute for Human Development in Berlin. She studies reforms in middle and high school science teaching, exploring different ways that teachers can be supported to improve their teaching practice and how this relates to student learning. She lives in Golden, Colorado, with her husband and two young children, and spends a fair amount of her free time trying to have a sense of humor about her profession.

Ian Parker Renga is a doctoral candidate in the School of Education at the University of Colorado at Boulder. He earned a BS in biology and BA in fine art from Indiana University (2001) and a master's degree in education from Harvard University (2005). Before returning to graduate school to study teaching and teacher education, he was a special needs paraeducator in Bellingham, Washington, and a middle school science and math teacher in Blacksburg, Virginia. He and his wife, Katie, and their dog, Tumble, live in Lafayette, Colorado.

CONTRIBUTORS

Troy Appling earned his PhD in English from Florida State University in 2010. While a teaching assistant in the first-year writing program at FSU, and later as an adjunct instructor at Santa Fe College in Gainesville, Florida, he tried to instill in his students the concept that citations are more than just getting commas and parentheses in the right place but also about giving credit where it is due and about joining your voice to a larger academic community. Upon completion of his dissertation on religious imagery in modern American drama, he accepted a tenure-track position at Florida Gateway College in Lake City, Florida, where he is now associate professor of English. He teaches Freshman Composition, Freshman Writing about Literature, American and World Literature Surveys, and Magazine Journalism.

Heather M. Bandeen is a current faculty member in Education Foundations at Inver Hills Community College in Minnesota. Before that she served as a visiting assistant professor in Evergreen State College's Master in Teaching (MiT) Program. Heather received her PhD from Ohio State University, MA from the University of Michigan, and BA from Michigan State University. She still has a soft spot for chocolate frosting.

Scott Dimovitz is associate professor of English at Regis University in Denver, Colorado. He specializes in twentieth- and twenty-first-century British literature, postmodern literature, and postcolonial literature and theory. He received his MA and PhD from New York University, and his articles have appeared in *LIT*, *Genre*, *MFS*, and *Studies in the Novel*. He is completing a manuscript on the works of Angela Carter.

Rick Anthony Furtak is associate professor of philosophy at Colorado College. He holds a BA in philosophy and English from Boston University and a PhD in philosophy from the University of Chicago. His philosophical interests include the moral psychology of the emotions, the relations between philosophy and literature, and the tradition of existential thought (especially Søren Kierkegaard and his legacy).

ABOUT THE EDITORS AND CONTRIBUTORS

Logan Greene is associate professor of English at Eastern Washington University. She taught composition as an adjunct at community colleges for about fifteen years, while also working full-time jobs. She worked in human resources for the New Mexico National Guard for ten years. She left that job in 1998 to enter the doctoral program at the University of New Mexico. She is married with two adult daughters and one granddaughter.

Amanda Jansen is mathematics educator and associate professor in the School of Education at the University of Delaware. She earned her PhD in educational psychology in 2004 from Michigan State University. When she is not researching students' engagement in school mathematics or studying how people learn to improve their mathematics teaching, she can be found behind the lens of her camera trying to see the world in new ways. Mandy has turned her research into "me-search" in at least one instance: through studying students' participation in mathematics classrooms, she has learned about ways that students attempt to achieve social goals and academic goals concurrently in classroom settings. This feels eerily familiar as Mandy has found most of her own friends through her academic workplace.

Hindi Krinsky is a doctoral candidate and teacher at Rutgers University, New Brunswick. Her work focuses on the incorporation of youth culture within the mainstream classroom. She is also the mom of two-year-old triplets: Ellie, Judy, and Ezra.

Julie C. Mitchell is associate professor of mathematics and biochemistry at the University of Wisconsin, Madison. Julie's research develops mathematical models for protein structure, focusing on the impact of mutations upon protein interactions. She received her PhD in mathematics from the University of California at Berkeley, after which she did postdoctoral studies in computational biology at the University of California at San Diego. Julie grew up in San Jose, California, in the days when it was a mixture of tech companies, family farms, and suburban sprawl. As a result, she loves computers and vegetables while hating the suburbs. In her spare time, Julie enjoys modern art, loud music, and fast cars.

ABOUT THE EDITORS AND CONTRIBUTORS

Lara Narcisi is associate professor of English at Regis University in Denver, Colorado. Her areas of specialization are twentieth- to twenty-first-century American literature, multiculturalism, and literary theory. She graduated from Yale cum laude, with distinction in the English major, in 1998. She received her MA and PhD from New York University and earned the school's university-wide Golden Dozen teaching award in 2003. Her articles have been published in such journals as *MELUS* and *Southern Studies*, and her book chapter on Sherman Alexie appears in *American Indians and Popular Culture*.

Steve Newton is associate professor of English at William Paterson University in Wayne, New Jersey. He was a Fulbright Scholar in 2005–2006 in the Institute for American Studies at the University of Graz in Graz, Austria. As a younger man he pumped gas in Alamosa, Colorado; drove a forklift in a cement factory in Cleveland, Ohio; was a nightshift janitor at the Grand Ole Opry; played guitar at a dude ranch in the southern Adirondacks; and one memorable Christmas was Santa Claus in a shopping mall outside Nashville.

Andrew Shtulman is associate professor of psychology and cognitive science at Occidental College in Los Angeles. He received a BA in psychology from Princeton University in 2001 and a PhD in psychology from Harvard University in 2006. His research focuses on conceptual development and conceptual change, particularly as they relate to science education. Shtulman is a leading expert on how children reason about physical possibility and how students misunderstand evolution by natural selection. Why the world needs an expert on these topics is not a question he likes to be asked.

Jessalynn Strauss is assistant professor of strategic communications at Elon University. She began a master's program at the University of North Carolina in 2002 with the intention of being a PR practitioner or possibly a sports writer. After graduating with her master's and working for two years, Jessalynn returned to school in 2006 to begin her PhD. In 1993, her high school physics teacher told her she should "think about being a teacher someday." She's glad she took his advice.

www.ingramcontent.com/pod-product-compliance
Lightning Source LLC
Chambersburg PA
CBHW070334230426
43663CB00011B/2312